MANAGING THE POOR PERFORMER

This book is dedicated to W.E. Hayward, Headmaster, an educator of much grace and breadth of vision.

Managing the Poor Performer

VALERIE STEWART
ANDREW STEWART

Gower

Published by
Gower Publishing Company Limited
Gower House, Croft Road, Aldershot, Hants GU11 3HR

Reprinted 1983
Revised and reprinted 1985, 1988, 2002

British Library Cataloguing in Publication Data

Stewart, Valerie
  Managing the poor performer.
  1. Employees, Rating of
  I. Title   II. Stewart, Andrew
  658.3'125   HF5549.5.R3

  ISBN 0 7045 0594 0

Typeset by Inforum Ltd, Portsmouth
Printed and bound in Great Britain by
Biddles Ltd, Guildford and King's Lynn

Contents

Preface

This book is written for the manager who has working for him one or two people whose performance is unsatisfactory. It has very limited aims – to help him take action to improve that performance so that it meets acceptable standards. It does not deal with the procedures you should go through if you want to fire him, or use the formal disciplinary procedure – there are good books to tell you about the law, and there are doubtless thick manuals from your personnel department to tell you what you may do in using the disciplinary process. No, this book is about what can and should happen between the two of you as people – between a manager and subordinate, in the regular management relationship, where you want to help him improve.

The book grew out of two pressures. The first was that we noticed on courses on various aspects of management that trainers would go carefully around the room collecting people's problems. When they came to problems of managing ineffective performance, they would usually dodge the issue. Often it would be the single unsatisfied need remaining at the end of an otherwise first-rate management course or seminar. And the second pressure came when we were writing our book *Practical Performance Appraisal* (Gower, 1978). When we prepared the chapter outlines we included a chapter on problem performers – the people who are thrown into relief by the appraisal system because they have a job problem. Obviously, we thought, any book on appraisal systems should have a chapter on its misfits. Then we looked around our library to see what other people had written about problem performers, and poor performers in particular, and found only one chapter specifically devoted to the subject – in Dunnette's *Handbook of Industrial and Organisational Psychology* (Rand McNally, 1976). This is a summary of experience in the field of poor performance, and while an excellent review of other people's work and a good indication of the main problems, it is not meant to be a practical guide for line managers. So, responding to the pressures, we sat down at the typewriter.

You might ask what our qualifications are to write such a book, and in this respect we are quite different from each other. When Andrew Stewart was a manager he had to cope with several cases of poor performance, and in each case managed to turn the situation round. (This is Valerie Stewart writing – we tossed a coin for it.) Valerie Stewart, on the other hand, boasts with many other fine people the distinction of having been fired for poor performance. In the long run, it hasn't done me any harm; without that experience I might even today be the deputy administrator in an infant school or spearheading the payroll function in some splendid office block. More seriously, we have written this book in large part through observing good managers at work – too many to acknowledge here, though one or two deserve a special mention or a book to themselves one day. Colin Hogg, of British Rail's Eastern Region, was responsible for a continuing performance improvement programme on the passenger side which involved many individual cases of marginal performance turned round; he put his faith behind some new techniques which are beginning to pay off handsomely. He has been a continuing delight to work with and learn from. And John Carlisle, of the Huthwaite Research Group, will recognise in these pages some of his ideas, and some of his own ways of making them memorable. He too has been a great help in systematising our thoughts and we acknowledge his help and hope he will be flattered by the plagiarism.

The book is arranged in three parts; the first part covers detecting poor performance, the second deals with the causes, and the third part describes ways of curing the problem. We have probably over-simplified to some extent, by taking causes singly and cures singly; any performance problem probably has a number of causes and may need two or three different approaches to improvement. We hope the reader will forgive and bear these points in mind: they do not alter the analysis of individual causes or remedies, just allow them to be described more clearly. Finally, as ever, our thanks to our editor Malcolm Stern at Gower, for his faith and tolerance, and to all those people whose experience has gone into the making of this book.

Valerie Stewart
Andrew Stewart

August 1981

Introduction

This book is about managing the poor performer. It assumes that the reader – a manager, or someone who has to advise managers – has working for him someone whose performance is not up to standard. The advice of this book – a distillation of some years of watching good man-managers at work – is designed to help the manager lift the poor performer from below the line to on-line. It's not designed to help you create superstars, nor is it designed to help you fire people. Nor is it a book designed to help you pull round a whole department or a whole company – to do this we would need to cover areas of management skill other than just the man-management skills discussed here. Nonetheless, we hope for quite a wide readership – there are plenty of managers who, looking at their team of people, can identify one or two who cost more to employ than they give back in results.

By concentrating on the middle of the job sandwich – i.e. pulling up a current poor performer – we ignore the two outside layers of recruitment and separation. This is largely because these topics are well treated elsewhere, but a brief word on them here is appropriate because (a) prevention is better than cure, and (b) you need to know what your options are if all your efforts look doomed to failure.

Recruitment

To do recruitment right you need to treat it like any other investment decision. If you recruit a blue-collar semi-skilled worker it'll probably take a minimum of six weeks before he starts to earn money for you – all the previous time is spent paying back the costs of recruiting him. Recruiting for the kind of job where people take months to play themselves in involves correspondingly greater opportunity costs if things go wrong. And yet people still persist in taking recruitment decisions with less thought than they give to ordering a good dinner. 'I don't have to bother with man-specifications, I'll recognise the right

1

man when I see him', says the manager who, when the new hire leaves because of a selection error, will accuse him of lack of 'stickability'. Many cases of poor performance can be traced back to poor selection, often coupled with poor induction training. A few pages reviewing the steps to be taken before making an appointment may help the rest of the book become a matter of less urgent interest to some readers.

Before you recruit you need a *job description* and a *person-specification*. Your company may already have its own set pattern of laying out these documents – there's no one right way. Some organisations write job descriptions using the three headings tasks, responsibilities, accountabilities; others use the system appropriate to their own job evaluation scheme. We believe that for writing job descriptions of managerial and senior specialist jobs there is no better guide than Rosemary Stewart's *Contrasts in Management* (McGraw-Hill, 1976): her breakdown of the factors into relationships, work pattern, exposure, choices, demands, and constraints is remarkably sensitive to life in the real world and also makes clear how one manages the leap from job description to person specification.

The person-specification should tell you what sort of experience, knowledge, and skills you want in your applicant. Break it down under those three headings, and be sure to make it clear how each part of your person-specification relates to the job description. If you write 'Must be an MBA from a good business school', for example, check that this is not just an irrational preference: why are MBAs from good business schools more likely to meet the requirements of the job description?

Now you have your person-specification, and you should be in a position to choose the selection method most appropriate to the task in hand. There is one other consideration to be borne in mind here – the supply of applicants suitable for the job. If of every fifty applicants forty-eight can do the job you don't really need a sophisticated selection device. If only one of the fifty could do the job, and any of the other forty-nine could cost a lot to recover, then you need to tread more carefully.

What selection methods are open to you? In roughly increasing order of complexity they are:

the personal history form
the one-man selection interview
the panel selection interview

psychological tests of aptitude/ability
psychological tests of personality/attitude
group selection techniques.

Faults with any of these could lead to problem performers later on. The most serious errors with each of these methods are set out below.

Personal history form. Quite simply, most organisations make poor use of their personal history forms. They are rarely designed with a particular job or range of jobs in mind. Some collect reams of information, most of which will not be used; others use two or three open questions with little guidance to the applicant and none to the end user. For an important one-off job, or a specialist function, it's probably worth designing an application form dedicated to that particular job. And it's certainly worth looking at your personal history forms and asking what they tell you that's useful and relevant to the task in hand.

The one-man selection interview is probably the single most misused part of the man-manager's equipment. Everybody reads articles and books reiterating the evidence that has accumulated since the beginning of this century showing that the unstructured interview has zero reliability – and everybody believes it of his neighbour, but not of himself. There are three things that no man will admit to doing badly, the story goes: driving a car, making love, and spotting the right man for the job. Yet the one-man selection interview plays some part in the recruitment process for nearly all appointments. Someone has to see the applicant; both parties need to ask questions. To make sure that the selection interview does what it can do well, and does no harm, observe the following rules:

1. Have a structure for the interview – decide in advance what areas you want to cover, how you will cover them, and how you will record the results.
2. Remember that the interview is better at telling you what the applicant has done in the past, and about his verbal skills; it is much less good at telling you about his personality and motivation, skills with peers and subordinates, and number of mechanical skills.
3. Remember that first impressions can have a devastating effect on your ability to form judgements later. Some research suggests that the average interviewer makes up

his mind in the first ninety seconds and then spends the rest of the time selectively gathering information to support his judgement.

The panel selection interview presents the opportunities and the threats of the one-man interview, only multiplied. An unstructured panel interview can do more damage to a firm's viability than a wild-cat strike. It's particularly difficult where the panel work as a panel over a period of time – then they become more resistant to the notion that they should agree responsibilities for particular areas of investigation. On the other hand, a structured panel interview that knows its own limitations, that assigns responsibilities for particular areas of investigation to particular people, that asks the panel to record their judgements individually on common forms before they negotiate a joint view – that sort of panel stands more chance of succeeding.

Psychological tests of aptitude and ability are useful because they add a qualitatively different area of knowledge about the candidate. The personal history form and the interview ask him to talk about his work; tests of ability and aptitude actually collect a work sample. But the tests need to be validated before you can rely on them. Someone needs to be able to demonstrate (a) that the test distinguishes accurately between people presently employed, with good job performers doing significantly better than poor job performers; and (b) if the test has been in use some time, that success in the job is significantly related to success on the test. This validation process needs to happen in your own firm. You should never buy a test that has been validated elsewhere – people will try to sell you such things but don't be tempted to buy. A test that is not supported by an in-house research programme is worse than no test, because its apparent objectivity means that people are less likely to question it.

The other common mistake with the use of tests is to make them more important than they should be in the decision-making process. They are only one item of information. If all else looks good and the test result looks poor, don't automatically throw the candidate out without further thought.

Psychological tests of personality and attitude add another dimension again to what you can learn in the selection process. But because these are complex topics the use to which these tests are put needs to be strictly controlled. The point about validation applies here just as much as previously, but with additional features; for it is possible to use personality tests to get a 'profile' of the typical effective job performer and try to recruit to that profile, *or* it is possible to take the profile of a particular applicant and ask: 'How would he cope in the job we have on offer?' The latter view – person-centred rather than job-centred – is finding more favour as it usually generates much more useful information; but it depends for success on having good job descriptions, a highly competent psychologist or trained person to interpret the tests, the use of well-researched tests and and in-house research programme.

Tests without the required back-up of published research are dangerous. A testing programme that does not guarantee security of the data is dangerous. Tests given to untrained people to interpret are dangerous. But tests properly used will tell you at selection time things you would otherwise have had to wait months to find out.

Group selection techniques, usually a half- or one-day variant on the management assessment programme, assemble a group of candidates together and give them one or two tasks to perform as a group, with observers looking on. Frequently the observers will be responsible for making the selection decisions. Again, the group selection techniques give you a chance to learn something that other selection methods do not offer – you see the candidates' interpersonal skills, their speed of comprehension of problems, their ability to cope under complex demands, etc. The opportunities for failure lie chiefly in the selection of the tasks and the training of the observers. The tasks people are given to do must be genuinely relevant to the job. So often one sees the observers having a quick colloquy five minutes before the start, after which one of them says: 'We'd like you to discuss what can be done to bring the world out of recession.' But even a relevant task or tasks can be misused if the observers themselves are not given a schedule to observe to; trained to observe to this schedule; trained to separate their observations from their evaluations; and checked for their consistency with each other.

Recruiting people is an investment decision, and like any other investment decision you need to decide what you want, the purpose for which you want it, and the methods you will use to test the quality of the material you are offered. If you can trace some of your problems with poor performers to poor selection techniques – yours or someone else's – then as well as dealing with your present problem you should try to prevent future ones.

Separation

That most people find this a painful topic to contemplate is supported by the large number of euphemisms in existence for firing someone. 'De-hire' is fairly common; 'No, we're not firing you, we're just de-committing from our recruitment decision,' says the manager in the cartoon, and we can all sympathise with his need to hide the unpleasant fact behind a screen of words. Employment legislation in the western world has made it much more difficult to fire people lately. Not that being a hire and fire employer has previously been easy; get yourself a bad reputation in the labour market and it becomes less and less easy to recruit high calibre staff. The legislation covering this topic changes quickly, and this book is not the place even to attempt an outline; suffice it to say that before tackling the problem of a poor performer the manager should familiarise himself with the law and with local procedures. Otherwise he may find himself unwittingly in the trap of having given a formal/informal, written/unwritten, first/second/third warning without knowing it. Really this book is about what to do to prevent your ever having to get to the stage of a formal warning, because as soon as such matters are raised things become dreadfully wary and legalistic; but you need to know where the cracks in the ice are so that you can plan to skate somewhere else.

What is poor performance anyway?

Part II of this book sets out a variety of reasons why people do not perform well at work. It is rarely due to simple bloody-minded indolence – anyway, that's a symptom, not a cause. We honestly believe that nobody starts his working life wanting to do a bad job. We also believe that nearly everybody could, at some time in his life, be judged a poor performer by some criteria. Most people have at some time been thrown in at the deep end to a job they did not know how to do; or suffered post-flu depression, post-childbirth depression, or some other undermining of the personality by the hormones; or found

themselves working for a series of superiors who pulled different ways and exerted different standards. If you climb out – with
or without assistance – you stop being a poor performer. But you
surely didn't want to start out as a poor performer.

Most cases of poor performance are multi-causal (and to that
extent we are guilty of over-simplification by isolating individual
causes later in this book). First one thing goes wrong, then
another. Maybe the boss or the poor performer doesn't realise
that things have started to slide, so neither party tries to correct
things until the poor performance has become a habit. Habits
are hard to correct, even when they are obviously bad for us –
ask any overweight nail-biting smoker with an overdraft. And
when you realise that you have become a poor performer and
want to change, the multi-causality of the problem makes it
difficult to know where to start. So it becomes easier to relapse.
Poor performance is expected of you in a way – you become the
group clown, the team dumbo, the tail-end Charlie. You have a
lot of expectations to satisfy – your own included – and to
improve now would be to run the risk of shattering some of
them. So you stay in the rut.

That's how it happens in most cases. For every poor performer you have because his Mum's a member of the Workers'
Revolutionary Party and has sent him to work to smash capital-
ism you've got twenty who slid into it almost without knowing.
So this book is not about blaming, but about understanding and
offering help.

There's a common fallacy in the applied sciences – including
medicine and psychology – that if you have diagnosed the cause
of a problem it is a simple matter to remedy it. You somehow
reverse the signs and the equation starts flowing in the other
direction. You can see this fallacy at work most clearly in
medicine, where students spend much more time learning how
to diagnose disease than learning how to cure it. Management
consultants are often guilty of thinking in this way. They will
give you a very expensive diagnosis of your problem, complete
with maps, diagrams, and the news that there's a lot of it about –
but usually won't tell you what to do to get rid of it. Try not to get
seduced by this model when you're looking at your poor performer. It is important to know the causes of the poor performance: then you can make a rough guess at the appropriate
remedy, and you can start a programme of prevention if the

problem occurs regularly; but there comes a time in the investigation process when you must look to the future, and you must deal with the problem you have on hand at the moment. You might not be able to reach back in history and reverse the switches on the original causes; that doesn't stop you from working out what to do next.

In Part III of this book we suggest various ways of coping with poor performance and pulling it up to standard. Some of the methods are more suitable to particular performance problems or particular personality types. People are individuals, and it needs your judgement, as the informed man on the spot, to decide how to approach any one case. However, with a multi-causal problem – or a multi-aspect problem, a problem that shows itself in several areas of job performance – you yourself may be faced with the problem: where do I start?

It's like unravelling a ball of tangled string. You look at the appalling mess, curse the cat, and turn the tangle over in your hand pulling at it. It doesn't matter how tangled it is, there is always one part of the bundle that is easier to shift than the rest. And this is where you start when you're undoing the tangle – and it's where you start when you're dealing with your problem performer. Take one or two easy bits first. Give him – and yourself – a record of early success. Convince yourselves that it can be done. Then go on with fresh confidence to tackle some of the more deepseated problems. If you attack these head on at the beginning you and he will get discouraged. Find the knot that is easiest to undo, and start there.

PART I
DETECTION

1 How do you know when someone is falling down on the job?

Detecting poor performance is easier in some jobs than in others. It is commonly said that doctors are able to bury their mistakes. A mistake in a spot-weld, or poor supervision around the concrete mixer, may not show up for years. If your salesman loses a sale by annoying or upsetting the customer, the commotion may alert you if you're in the vicinity; if on the other hand he loses sales because he does not question the customers properly to find out their needs you may never know what he is doing wrong.

Industries have their own patterns of poor performance. Railway guards and miners are more likely to go absent, especially on Mondays; milkmen typically have a lower absenteeism level, but if they don't do well in the job they leave. The degree of internal competitiveness appropriate in some American organisations would be regarded as deliberate trouble-making by many British managers. To make an appointment for 18.30 on Friday evening is considered a sign of success in one organisation and a sign of failure in another.

Detecting poor performance is not always as easy as it may seem. But any checklist of things to look for must cover the following:

1. *Quantity of work*. Is the worker doing as much work as the average for this firm? Is he doing significantly less? Is he doing significantly more and thus risking becoming a workaholic, a non-delegator, an indispensable over-worked hero? What factors influence the amount of work he can do – is he a trainee, unfit, part-time? How much control does he have over the amount of work he can do?
2. *Quality of work*. Is the worker producing to the appropriate quality standards? If he is not, is there any pattern to his lack of quality – are there typically any areas which he skimps or overlooks?
3. *Abseenteeism*. Is the worker habitually absent from work? Are the absences supported by notes from the doctor? Are

the medical reasons given likely to be true, or have they been provided by a harassed doctor who simply accepts what the worker chooses to tell him? Are there patterns to the absenteeism associated with, for instance, local sporting events, work tasks, particular days of the week?

4. *Other forms of withdrawal from work*. Does the worker seem to be particularly accident-prone? Does he stick at jobs, or drift from one to another? Is he continually on the internal transfer list? Does he arrive late and go home early? Does he stretch his tea-breaks to the maximum and beyond? Does he make other people waste their time, by indulging in social chit-chat whenever anyone shows any signs of taking their work seriously?

5. *Conflict*. Does the worker appear to provoke a lot of quarrels? Do people seem reluctant to work with him? Do members of the public with whom he comes into contact complain about his behaviour? Does he always have ten reasons for not taking action and none for doing anything? Is he a 'stirrer'?

6. *Dishonesty*. Does he fiddle his expenses? Pinch from the till? Call relatives in Australia on the firm's telephone? Steal from the customers? Take bribes?

7. *Refusal to volunteer*. Does he do the absolute minimum necessary to perform the job, but no more? Is he the shop assistant who hides the credit-card machine? The airline check-in clerk who won't tell you what time your flight boards? The bus driver who won't give change? The insurance salesman who doesn't explain to the customer that the policy he's taking out won't in fact meet his needs?

8. *Lack of delegation*. Is he the manager who doesn't trust his staff enough to delegate to them, and so finishes up with a staff who cannot handle the tasks anyway? Does he delegate 'only those things I don't have time to do myself'? Does he delegate under protest and take things back the minute anyone makes a mistake or the timing slips slightly?

9. *Unrealistic targets*. Does he set for himself targets that are so easy he will be certain to meet them, or so difficult that he can't be blamed if he misses them?

10. *Information distortion*. Does he want to be told the good news, but ignore or punish people who bring him bad news?

11. *Slow decisions*. Does he avoid taking decisions? Does he

manufacture pseudo-problems to give himself something to do which distracts from the real decisions – like the Watergate conspirators who had top-level meetings about the colour of the White House pencils and whether to have biodegradable cups by the water fountains?

12. *Capriciousness*. Does he play practical jokes? Womanise? Keep everyone up late at night on courses so they're no good the following morning? Get drunk a lot?

Obviously we are not suggesting that one practical joke, or one dispute with the boss, turns someone into a poor performer. But most managers who ask advice on how to deal with poor performers name one or more of the above factors, *carried on for some length of time*, as the cause of their concern.

One thing we should make clear from the beginning is that we are discussing *performance*; in other words, how people behave at work. Our concern is with what people do, not with what they are. The reason is twofold: firstly, that it's much easier to change what people do than to change their personality, and secondly that if you as the employer try to change someone's personality then you're trespassing on his identity outside work – into the areas of his family, friends, outside interests – and ethically you should not do that without permission. Obviously personality factors do influence performance at work, but the best time to negotiate at the level of personality is when you are appointing someone to a job, so that you stand some chance of getting the kind of person you need.

There are, however, areas on the borderline of performance, which cause much heart-searching. One such is *appearance*: are staff who refuse to wear the prescribed uniform poor performers? Staff who are untidy? Staff with long hair? Another such bothersome area is the one managers and supervisors sometimes call 'presentability' when they think of staff who have to meet the public. Here they have in mind questions like: should the staff smile, smoke, eat, stay seated, call women 'madam' or 'dear', use the customer's name, help with parcels. As customers we can probably all recall occasions when staff who did not meet these standards lost our goodwill; and as managers we can surely sympathise with the difficulty the supervisors must have when they try to make such standards seem objective and relevant to business success.

The test in these borderline areas must be one of reasonableness. H.J. Heinz could insist on having no salesman less than six feet tall; today, though, he would have to submit that performance criterion to the test of whether reasonable men would agree that non-compliance would have a deleterious effect on the business.

We are concerned in this book with the problems of the manager or supervisor who has one or two people working for him who are performing badly. But we must not ignore the issues that arise when the whole organisation is performing badly, where an inappropriate organisational culture swamps the manager's objective judgement of what is good or bad. (In other words, we are limiting ourselves to considering the problems of one or two bad apples in the barrel, and not with what you do when the whole orchard's got blight.) An item in *The Times* diary for 1 July 1980, is a good illustration of what we mean:

Vim Vs. Verbiage

The British civil servant loves commiteemanship. He places the art of drafting on a pedestal. Style is as important as content.

One Whitehall veteran of economic summitry returned from Venice brimming with praise for the chairmanship of the Italian Prime Minister, Signor Cosiga, and the wording of the resulting communiqué 'at which the Italians had had the first stab.'

So much better, he added, than the Tokyo summit last year where, at both ministerial and official level, meetings had been lacking in direction because the Japanese, who were in the chair, knew nothing about the beloved skills of chairmanship and draftsmanship.

If the relative performance of our own and the Italian economy is any guide, our Far Eastern friends are better off without them. While our politicians and civil servants preside with charm and impeccable phraseology over a shrinking economic base, the non-committee types in Tokyo flood the British market with cars and electronic equipment, not one carburettor or transistor of which owes a thing to a crisp agenda or an agreed report.

Perhaps the Civil Service is, in present-day Britain, too obvious a target for assaults on its performance criteria. There are many other organisations that could use a severe dose of informed introspection about their strategy and the working environment they provide before their managers start to blame individual employees for poor performance. If the organisation as a whole is performing badly then action and advice are needed which are outside the scope of this book; but before he starts to criticise other people's performance the manager should try to make sure that he is not applying idiosyncratic standards, or criticising an employee for perfomance that shines out like a good deed in a naughty world. A useful discipline is to ask oneself the following questions:

1. *Exactly what behaviour* is it that I am objecting to? If I had to capture the poor performance on film what would I point my camera at? If I could show him to an invisible observer, what unsatisfactory features of his work would I want to point out?

2. *How does this behaviour* adversely affect our business? Can I make out a reasonable case that it is costing us money, or effort, or time, that would be better spent elsewhere?

3. *Would any other manager* or supervisor be likely to see the same poor performance as I see and interpret it in the same way, or am I being eccentric?

4. *Am I over-generalising* on too little evidence, or on the basis of small traits that I dislike? Do I think that people with untidy desks automatically have untidy minds, or that no-one with long hair should be allowed to serve the public?

If the answers are reasonably satisfactory – in other words, you are confident that you are dealing with a real problem and not one of your own imagining – then you should be able to answer the toughest question of all:

5. *Could I defend* my judgement at an industrial tribunal if the worker's behaviour deteriorated to the point where dismissal became my only course of action?

One final preparation for the manager about to confront the problem of poor performance. It's useful to meditate on the large number of successful businessmen who have significant or even massive failures behind them. Many companies have proved unable to evaluate the potential of money-making ideas (xerography, the hovercraft, the whole-body scanner). People who have never made mistakes are deadly dull. Your poor performer could have it in him to become a really high-flyer, if you offer good disinterested help. And there but for the grace of God goes . . . well, just about everybody.

2 How can the organisation help managers detect poor performance?

Some organisations provide methods to help the manager detect poor performance. These may take the form of systems designed to highlight problem areas, or they may consist of training the managers to analyse performance better. Obviously a really poor performance will stand out on its own; but the sub-critical performance, the slowly deteriorating one, or the performance where results come too late to take corrective action, may be more difficult to detect. Maybe also the responsible manager does not see the people very often, leaving the day-to-day control in the hands of a supervisor who is not empowered to take any action. Many retail chains and round-the-clock businesses work like this; the power of the immediate supervisor is very limited and initiatives to improve poor performance must come from the next level up.

We classify the methods organisations provide into three groups: checks against existing standards, challenges to the conventional wisdom, and outside views.

Checks against existing standards

In these methods the organisation provides a set of job-related criteria against which the performance of individual people or departments is reviewed on a regular basis. The most obvious example of this is the performance appraisal system. Other examples are the call reporting systems designed for salesmen or service engineers to report on their activities; analysis of customer complaint letters, quality control checks, analysis of scrap rates, budgetary controls, etc. We shall look at two examples here:

Performance appraisal systems
The performance appraisal system of any organisation can be described using one or more boxes in the following diagram

17

	overt	covert
control		
maintenance		
development		

It is a sad accident that the widespread interest in performance appraisal systems which sprang up in the 1960s and early 1970s coincided with what seems – looking back through rose-coloured spectacles – to have been a period of smooth industrial expansion and related assumptions about growth. Many appraisal systems designed then were overtly about development, even if the covert purposes were different. Only in avowedly bureaucratic organisations, where it is more important that everyone perform to a given standard than that some people excel, will you find the overt purpose to be 'control'; a 'controlling' system is easily identified by the fact that individual development is constrained by a ruling that no-one may see his performance appraisal unless it is unsatisfactory.

Most appraisal systems exert some degree of control by providing the opportunity for the appraiser to record that the appraisee's performance has been unsatisfactory. For example, a rating scale in increasingly common use is the following:

A – excellent, outstanding
B – exceeds requirements in most respects
C – exceeds requirements in some respects
D – meets basic job requirements
E – fails to meet basic job requirements

and an appraisee whose performance was classed as E would be taken out of the regular appraisal system and put into a formal warning/remedial category. We have written elsewhere about the design, installation, and maintenance of appraisal systems (see p.175) and will not repeat ourselves here. There are however some specific points about the use of the performance appraisal system for detecting poor performance:

1. Where the appraisal system is used *primarily* for the detection and discipline of poor performers the rest of the employees will become restive. Where no-one but poor performers have the results of their appraisals communicated to

them the system veers close to the 'disciplinary' end of the continuum. In the British Civil Service, for example, where this rule applies, many managers risk the opprobrium of the personnel department and show the results of their appraisals to all staff, in order to maintain morale which they value highly.

2. Where the appraisal system exists *overtly* for purposes of development or maintenance but is used covertly for control, it entails the same risks as described above, with the added difficulty which always arises when a managerial tool is used hypocritically. A good way of testing whether there is this division between overt and covert purposes is to compare the speed with which things happen as a result of the appraisal programme. If training needs for moderate and good staff get ignored, while head office leans on 'D' performers, there may be some tension here.

3. Where the appraisal system is used for control purposes and salary rises follow closely on appraisals the open quality of the appraisal interview will suffer. No-one is going to talk freely about his strengths and weaknesses if it costs him £50 per weakness.

In many ways one could wish that the problem of poor performers were totally separate from the appraisal system which is (or should largely be) about different things. However, the letter or the spirit of much employment law says otherwise. It is important therefore to recognise the particular but limited role the appraisal system can play in detecting poor performance and to make sure that its possibilities and limitations are communicated to the people who must use it.

Analysis of historical data
Analysis of customer complaints will often reveal areas of poor performance. So will analysis of scrap rates, returned goods, repeat service calls, costs and budgeting. The following guidelines need to be observed, though, before you can be sure you are getting a true picture of the poorly-performing people:

1. The analysis categories need to be set to reveal what you want to know. For example, in British Rail, letters of complaint are filed under different headings; one is 'Late running trains', another 'Train cleanliness' and so on. These

categories were decided by the operators – the people who actually run the system. If you want to track down areas of individual poor performance you have to re-draw the categorisation system so as to catch data about the helpfulness of guards on late-running trains, the quality of information given to the people waiting, etc.

2. Data must be analysed, not just looked at for individual horrific incidents. Trends of poor performance, or poor performance sustained over a long time, should be worked on in preference to the person who does his work well most of the time but has made the odd appalling error. Besides being more likely to benefit from your help, the poor performer you have data about forms a better basis for your case if you have to defend yourself to the union or staff association.

3. Take care when apportioning blame. One person with a high scrap rate may be a poor performer; when the whole of the section has a high scrap rate the fault may lie with the supervisor; and when the whole of the shop has a high scrap rate it could be the fault of the person who designed the machines, the manager responsible for the shift system, or the person who did the training.

Challenges to the conventional wisdom

In these methods for detecting poor performance the common factor is that research has revealed that what people *say* is effective performance is not actually correlated with effective performance when more objective methods are used. For example, some firms have found that skilfully designed territory mangement diaries reveal that their salesman do not need training in making presentations or doing demonstrations, but would profit more from training in how to make appointments or how to write proposals. These issues become obvious once the managers are encouraged to examine the conversion ratios during the different stages in the sales cycle, and to compare these with the results obtained over the company as a whole. Again, objective studies of some negotiators have shown that the skills conventionally held in high esteem – tough-mindedness, a will to win, a 'mean streak' – are less important in some circumstances than qualities of analysis, honesty, far-sightedness, and the ability to leave the other party a bridge.

It is easy to deceive ourselves about what makes for successful behaviour. If we study economics we learn to predict the behaviour of 'economic man', ignoring the fact that most people don't actually behave like that. Similarly, theories of human behaviour encourage us to assume that people learn from their mistakes and would therefore like to hear about them fast. We assume that people will be consistent. It is all too easy to fall into the trap of assuming that A happening just before B is the same as A causing B. In the area of management a few experts like Peter Drucker and Charles Handy 'tell it like it is'; but most of us are victims of delusions which prevent our seeing the real areas where performance falls down.

One of the best founded challenges to the conventional wisdom comes in the area of selling, where the Huthwaite Research Group, led by Neil Rackham, have looked at what actually happens in sales calls and what differentiates between successful and less successful calls. The conventional wisdom here, of course, places a lot of emphasis on the importance of 'closing' the sale. The Huthwaite research showed by contrast that closing behaviour is slightly negatively linked to sales success except when the product on offer is so cheap that, in effect, the customer gives the salesman some money to go away. The Huthwaite research also showed that training salesmen in handling objections was largely a waste of effort, because a good salesman should never get himself into a state where objections were given.

Though the Huthwaite studies reveal that there is no fixed pattern which all successful sales calls follow, they did show that the successful salesmen asked questions – not any old questions, but four distinct kinds of question:

1. *Situation questions* – to learn something about the client's conditions and circumstances. Good salesmen usually ask a limited number of situation questions; it's possible to ask too few or too many, and inexperienced salesmen often ask nothing but situation questions.
2. *Problem questions* – to learn something about the kind of problems the client is currently experiencing. Poor salesmen often stop here, especially if their product knowledge is so great that they feel tempted to leap to the 'correct' product without pausing to develop the customer's needs.

3. *I*mplication questions – where the problems the client talks about are examined in more depth to encourage him to think about the implications they have for his business. While the first two kinds of question help to uncover 'implicit' needs, the process of asking implication questions begins to make these implicit needs explicit – and therefore more apparent, obvious, and painful to the client.

4. *N*eed-pay off questions – which ask the client to put a value of some sort on a solution to the problem.

To summarise so far, the Huthwaite research showed that poor salesmen asked few questions, often limited themselves to situation questions only, and did not develop implicit needs into explicit needs. They also found that how the product was described influenced whether a sale was made, distinguishing between three different ways of describing the product:

Features – attributes of the product
Advantages – how these attributes can be used to help the buyer
Benefits – how a product feature or advantage meets an explicit need expressed by the buyer.

Benefit statements are much more likely to lead to a sale. In their SPIN training programme (the acronym SPIN stands for the four different kinds of question contributing to the sale) Huthwaite equip managers with the skills to accompany their salesmen on sales visits and to analyse precisely where their performance needs help. Training modules – nearly always self-administered – are available for the salesman to work through to improve his performance in the defective areas.

The SPIN programme is a good example of a challenge to the conventional wisdom, based on research, and containing within itself assistance for the manager to take action on poor performance immediately.

Outside/long views

Under this heading we classify any input about standards or performance which comes from an informed outside source, or which is organised internally but on a deliberately disinterested basis. It is unusual for these methods to point to any one particular poor performer – by their very nature they would cease to be acceptable within the firm – but they may point to general areas where performance should be investigated further.

Outside consultants' reports

Many firms of consultants will survey an organisation's performance. They can be addressed to a specific closed question ('How much discretionary business are we losing?' 'How effective is our advertising?' 'Have we got any safety hazards?') or more open questions ('What should our organisational strategy be in the next fifteen years?' 'How can we improve the quality of our senior management?'). Some consultants volunteer to do an unpaid survey; chances are they'll want to recoup their costs by finding problems within their own area of competence. Others will survey for a fee. Rare ones will tell you when they think you don't have a problem. It is possible to use consultants to help define and improve poor performance. Before engaging the consultants, though, you should consider the following issues:

1. Are the consultants going to be invited to make judgements about the competence of individual people? If so, to whom will these judgements be communicated? Does this include the people themselves?
2. The consultants are bound to gather informal views about the competence of individual people. What policy will there be about the communication of this information?

It should go without saying that these decisions must be taken honestly and adhered to. The publication of PA Consultants' report about London Transport – apparently against the original expectations of many of the LT people themselves – reminds us that such a policy is not always followed. We have been asked sometimes to 'interview my board on a pretext of some kind and then give me a confidential report on how competent they are . . . how loyal they are . . . whether they're plotting to get rid of me.' One large American firm of consultants will in fact openly offer to perform this dubious service for a chief executive, and have launched some expensive reigns of terror to no good effect.

An outside consultant's report can be particularly valuable in helping to set standards of performance in areas where the existing management team is inexperienced; in bringing credibility to areas that have been neglected; and addressing perform-

ance problems at senior level. Outsiders can also be used as
professional counsellors to work directly with the problem performers, and can sometimes achieve more lasting change
because of their neutral standpoint.

Attitude surveys
Some firms conduct regular attitude surveys of their employees
in which job satisfaction, morale, working conditions, etc., are
examined. Others commission attitude surveys on a one-off
basis whenever a specific problem appears to loom large. Sometimes attitude surveys point to a performance problem – if all the
employees in one department report themselves as discontented
with their manager, for instance. Sometimes the feedback and
action planning cycle which should follow an attitude survey
uncovers problems locally which can be locally managed. Some
firms like IBM make their managers feed back the survey results
to their employees and plan joint action on problems. Others
like Scott Bader use an outside friend of the company to
perform this service. They use an industrial chaplain and claim
that this is extremely effective.

In summary, we have identified a number of ways in which
organisations help managers monitor performance standards.
The methods themselves need careful management, as they are
designed to look at the organisation as a whole and must not
become a vehicle for punishment or people will cease to cooperate with them. One rule in the management of poor performers, applicable to all methods of identifying them, is well
worth following:

> As soon as someone knows that he has been identified as a
> poor performer he should know that processes to put this
> right have been started.

PART II

UNDERSTANDING THE CAUSES

3 Abilities and job knowledge

Poor performance may be caused by lack of the abilities or lack of the knowledge necessary to do the job. Every one of us has been in that position at some time or another; indeed there is a school of thought which says that 'throwing a man in at the deep end' – putting him in a situation for which he is not equipped and seeing how quickly he learns to cope – is a good way of training and assessing potential. If the difference between his present abilities and the required abilities is the right size – enough to seem like a manageable challenge, not too much to be demoralising – this method can be effective. But the challenge must be correctly judged. Few people would learn to fly a space capsule by being put into the shoes of one of the Apollo-13 crew.

Deficiencies in ability or job knowledge can be grouped under the following heads:

Intelligence and related abilities

The structure of human intelligence is a fascinating study about which there are still considerable areas of ignorance. However, a generally accepted model of intelligence is that there is a general intelligence factor, often abbreviated as 'g'. The 'g' factor itself is difficult to define comprehensively, but a good broad definition is 'the ability to learn from experience'. Linked to the central 'g' factor are various specific factors, like verbal, mechanical, numerical and spatial abilities. A person can have quite a high score on one of these abilities and a low score on another. It's not uncommon to find someone in the top 10 per cent of the ability range for verbal intelligence and in only the top 40 per cent for numerical intelligence – or the other way around. So the brilliant engineer who performs badly in negotiations is not necessarily wilful or demotivated, he may just not have the verbal ability to match his numerical and spatial intelligence. And the brilliant administrator who lets slip a simple mathematical mistake may not be deliberately careless; perhaps he doesn't have the mathematical abilities to go with his general and verbal intelligence.

Every individual is a product of his heredity and his environment. You inherit from your parents a capability which does not
set a ceiling on your achievements, but rather defines a floor
below which you have no excuse for falling. Then the richness of
your early environment – how much stimulation there is, how
much variety in what you see and hear and touch and smell and
feel – affects the amount of your developing brain which gets
accustomed to being used. Intelligence and abilities develop
through childhood, into adolescence, and then start slowly to
decline. Some abilities, like the ability to hear very high frequency notes, begin declining in the late teens and early twen-
ties. However, psychologists have a strong suspicion that the
decline in many abilities which the older textbooks describe is
due not so much to inevitable physical deterioration as to sheer
lack of use. Practise your facilities, the message is, and you won't
lose them. The more intelligent people – as measured by tests –
generally find their abilities continue to develop later into life,
and start to decline later and less steeply. Older people are often
slower on intelligence tests, and take longer to learn new skills;
to compensate for that, many older people have learned to use
their experience and existing skills in a way that makes them at
least as useful as younger people. The statement 'This is a job for
a younger person' is rarely justified on grounds of intelligence
alone; only on assembly line work, where older people may
suffer because the pacing causes them problems, is one justified
in thinking that one might automatically debar people above a
certain age.

What are the implications for this for the manager? Why
should he need to know someone's intelligence to take corrective action on poor performance? How should he set about
finding out whether it is a contributory factor in someone's poor
performance?

Test general and specific abilities
Bearing in mind the brief outline of the structure of intelligence
given above, it should be obvious that knowing someone's general ability level without knowing some of the specifics is
unlikely to be helpful. This is particularly so when you have
someone performing badly after transferring from one job to
another even after time for settling in has been allowed. For

shopfloor and office workers a well-validated and widely-used test is the Differential Aptitude Test, which gives information on the following factors:

verbal reasoning
numerical ability
abstract reasoning
clerical speed and accuracy
mechanical reasoning
space relations
spelling
language usage.

Any or all of the factors may be tested. The test is often used for selection and placement decisions, particularly with school-leavers. It is very helpful in pinpointing exactly where specific difficulties may arise, so that a decision based on detailed information becomes possible. With adults of higher intelligence – graduate level population – a widely-respected test is the AH6 test of high intelligence, giving information on the following factors:

verbal ability
numerical ability
spatial ability

The AH6 exists in two forms: one for Arts and General population, in which numerical and spatial abilities are combined to give a single score, and the Scientists, Engineers and Mathematicians version, in which separate scores are given for all three abilities.

If, as a result of a test, you find that someone is lower on the particular abilities necessary to do the job than you had thought him to be, you may consider intensive training, job redesign, or putting the person into another job. It is unlikely that you will achieve very much change in basic abilities by training, however. If the tests reveal that the person does have the basic abilities to do the job, then you must look for an explanation in one of the factors covered by the later chapters.

'Too much' can be as bad as 'too little'
It is possible to perform poorly because the job is not demanding enough. A very bright person put into a dull job, with no

prospect of release, often does badly.

There are times when it is impossible to avoid putting a bright person into an undemanding job. Many graduate entry schemes, for example, demand that the graduate spend some of his time on the shopfloor or otherwise 'play himself in' in a job that is not of itself very demanding. In these cases it is important to make sure that the graduate accepts the frustration to his intellectual abilities and knows its place in his development scheme. A more difficult problem occurs when for status or other reasons people have been deliberately over-recruited. As we write, there are few jobs for graduates available. Some self-important employers have said that they will therefore take people only with first-class honours degrees, ignoring the reality of the jobs these people will go into – jobs which in some cases are not graduate level jobs at all. Similar examples of over-recruitment can be found at all levels of employee ability when jobs are scarce.

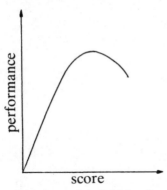

In one firm, we found that the relationship between success as a computer salesman and score on the Data Processing Aptitude Test was as described by the graph alongside; very high scoring people did not make good salesmen because they got too interested in the details of the system and didn't like handing over responsibility to the systems analysts. But we could not persuade the recruiting managers that this relationship meant that they should hire from the 'B' scorers when recruiting salesmen – 'Why should I take Bs when there are As available?' came the cry. In the end, we re-labelled the test results so that Bs did become As, and vice versa – with subsequent improvement in performance.

The problems of over-recruitment are more easily avoided than cured. If you suspect you have such a problem on your hands, it's worth trying to expand the person's job to see if he does any better as a result.

Use a validated test

In the UK there is no licensing system for psychologists or psychological tests. Anyone may call himself a psychologist, and anyone may market tests. You should ask to see the validation data before you use a test. At the moment the intelligence testing field is short of simple job-related tests of ability which are robust enough to be administered by recruiting managers out in the field – shop managers, switchboard supervisors, dairy managers, etc. The quick test which would enable the manager to tell whether the applicant stood a reasonable chance of being able to do a job – maybe a Saturday job or a temporary job where the expense of formal testing is not justified – would be very helpful, and more need to be developed.

In summary, then, poor job performance can be caused by a level of intelligence that is too low to do the job, or too high to want to do the job; and we should differentiate 'intelligence' into a group of related abilities which feed into a central core. When someone's intelligence is too low, he may just not be able to grasp what the job requires and learn the necessary skills; when it is very much too high, he may perform badly because the job does not challenge him enough. Where a previously good performer shows a decline on transfer to a new job demanding different abilities the poor performance may be due to someone over-generalising – 'He's good at X, so he's bound to be good at Y' – without realising that different abilities may be possessed to different degrees by the same person. Where a person seems to have the right abilities and not be too over-qualified, then the problem probably lies elsewhere.

Memory difficulties

Human beings have at least two kinds of memory – short-term and long-term. The short-term memory is a kind of holding store for the long-term memory; once information is out of the short-term memory into the long-term, it's very difficult to lose it. But information can be lost out of the short-term memory, and it's as if it had never been there. The following experiment will show what we mean.

Get a friend to read out to you the following lists of numbers. The numbers should be read at about one a second, without grouping them or giving them a rhythm. Your job is to say the list of numbers in time with your friend, only for the *first* list you must say the first number as the friend calls the second. For the *second* list you must wait until your friend reads the third

number before you give the first. For list three you must go 'four
back' and so on:

```
1   4   6   3   7   4   9   6
2   8   5   7   6   9   4   4
3   5   4   7   9   0   6   1
5   4   7   8   6   9   3   1
9   0   6   4   5   6   3   2
```

Difficult, isn't it? Trying to put things into the short-term memory and take them out again at the same time reveals how
limited the mechanism really is. In fact, psychologists generally
accept that for most people the biggest number of separate
pieces of information they can handle in the short-term memory
at one time is seven, plus or minus two. More than this magic
number $7+2$ and you don't notice, you forget, or you develop
strategies for grouping numbers of items together so that each
group becomes a unit. The relevance of this to poor performance? Simply that a lot of jobs are designed without reference
to the limitations of the short-term memory, and they overload
it. When the British Post Office introduced an all-figure dialling
code, in many cases using ten digits, people found telephone
numbers difficult to remember. 0213734807 is difficult to
remember as it stands. You have to group it – 021-373-4807 –
and most people know that 021 means Birmingham so they are
not dealing with three separate numbers, 0, 2 and 1, but with
one unit '021-means-Birmingham'.

   Any job that involves taking in information, storing it briefly,
and putting it out again is vulnerable to the effects of short-term
memory. Anyone who has to look up timetables and schedules
in response to requests is vulnerable. The person on the end of
the telephone who takes down orders from the salesman in the
field is vulnerable. The secretary taking down an assortment of
different messages is vulnerable.

   There are two strategies for coping with the bottleneck caused
by the short-term memory. The first is to learn to code information into manageable chunks, so that 021 becomes one chunk
and not three. The second is to design the job and/or perform it
in such a way that the short-term memory is not overloaded. For
example, we played the one-back, two-back, three-back memory game with travel clerks and while the lesson was fresh in
their minds helped them develop the rule: 'Never give more

than three pieces of schedule information at one time before giving the customer a chance to write it down.' They soon reported fewer 'Can you say that again?' 'I didn't quite catch all that' requests.

Once in the long-term memory, information is very difficult to lose completely though it may take a good deal of poking about to remember things from the really dim and distant past. Some people find that aids to memory are useful. The commonest aids are:

1. *Associations* – where you invent an association which will link the new information with the old. If your car registration number begins GPM it may help you in remembering that Geoff Phipps runs the Marketing department. Trying to remember that the Solihull plant makes washers, you tell yourself that every time you've been to Birmingham it's been raining.

2. *Mnemonics* – where you remember lists of information by forming a word or sound from the initial letter of the component parts. Proteins are made from CHOPSN (Carbon, Hydrogen, Oxygen, Phosphorus, Sulphur and Nitrogen). Taking charge of a group of soldiers, you must remember SMEACS (Situation, Mission, Execution, Administration, Command, Signals); giving orders to the ones with the guns, you must remember GRIT (Group, Range, Indicator, Target).

3. *Visual constructions* – where you deliberately build up visual associations to supplement the information taken in verbally. You might remember our description of intelligence better if you pictured it as a wheel, with 'g' factor at the centre and the specific factors radiating away from it. You may remember an argument better if you think of it as a computer flowchart.

From time to time books appear promising you a tremendous improvement in memory if you'll just follow the author's system. Mostly the books offer you variations on the theme of associations or mnemonics; and mostly the people who find these devices useful already have discovered this for themselves. People with memory difficulties may find the method of visual construction helpful; man is such a verbal animal that he forgets to use his other senses, and if you remember what information looks like as well as sounds like you may do better.

If you say of someone 'his memory's going', the first thing to look for is the demand the job makes on the short-term memory. The introduction of computers into office procedures often changes these demands. Remember how limited the short-term store is. If you have taken corrective action on the short-term memory, you're unlikely to encounter serious memory deficit unless the person is really getting on in years or has suffered brain damage or head injury.

Lack of job knowledge

People may perform badly because they lack the basic knowledge necessary to do the job well. Remember SMEACS? People need briefing under each of these headings before you can say they know enough to do the job well:

Situation – what kind of organisation do they work for, and where does their own department or function fit into the overall picture?

Mission – what are they there to achieve? What difference does it make whether they do their job properly? What do they contribute?

Execution – what, precisely, do they have to do? If a camera team were to record them doing the job, what would it need to capture the essence of the job on film?

Administration – what information will they need? What information will they generate? Who gets it, who keeps it, and why?

Command – who's in charge? Whom do they report to? What are the limits of their authority?

Signals – how, when, and by what means will they send and receive information, and who contacts whom?

That seems so obvious it shouldn't need saying. But how many jobs are assigned without clear terms of reference? 'I'd like you to liaise between Sales and Production on this one, Jack.' 'We're looking for a Management Development Officer, to be responsible for all management development in the engineering function.' 'The supervisor's sick, so will you stand in for him until he comes back?' 'Will you put together a task force to work on this problem?' If more managers made sure that they had got clear all the points covered by SMEACS before handing over, there would be fewer cases of poor performance because the parties disagreed about the job to be done.

Check that the poor performer knows what he's supposed to do, how he's supposed to do it, and what his relationships with the rest of the organisation are supposed to be. Don't assume that the company induction programme – if you have one – will have told him everything. Company induction programmes are a good thing, but you often need a departmental or local programme as well. Remember that some young employees may have missed the induction programme if you run it only for school-leavers or graduates in September and some people join in January. And make sure that the newcomer feels free to ask naive questions – often it can be months into a new job before you realise all the questions you should have asked on the first day.

To summarise: lack of basic abilities and job knowledge may cause poor performance if the abilities are undeveloped, insufficient, or too great; if the job has been designed so that no-one of ordinary human capacity could do it; or if the employer has not given the employee the specific briefing he needs to do the job well.

4   Stress and emotional problems

Stress can cause poor performance. This is an experience in reach of most of us, for most people have experienced at least minor forms of stress at work, as the following outline of the relationship between stress and motivation makes clear.

If we draw a graph showing the relationship between the motivation to do the task – any task – and the resulting standard of performance, it is in the form of an inverted U. For low levels of motivation, performance is of low standard. As the motivation increases the standard of performance approaches an optimum. Increased motivation past the optimum point actually brings the standard of performance down again.

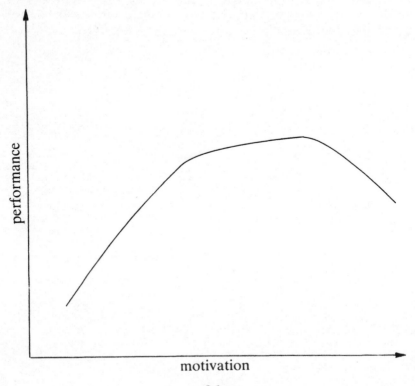

There are no units on the above graph, because the relationship is universal. It holds for any performance, and for any kind of motivation linked to producing that performance. It holds for everyone; some people peak earlier than others, some kinds of task and motivation peak earlier than others, but everyone is vulnerable to the effects of this law. It is, in fact, one of the few universal laws of behaviour that psychologists have been able to derive in all their years of studying the vagaries of the human animal.

While there are individual differences in the exact shape of the curve for different people and tasks, we know that complex tasks tend to peak earlier than simple ones. Encouragement from the foreman's boot may speed up the rate of digging, but is likely to disrupt the writing of a computer programme. Because environmental stimulation acts as a motivator, we sometimes find that people performing tasks of different complexity in the same environment experience the environment differently. The background music at airports may help the passengers at the same time as it disrupts the people working on ticket validation; the typist who listens to Radio 2 as she works could find that what helps her in her rather dull job is a positive hindrance to her boss trying to draw up the marketing plan.

If you understand this graph and think back to occasions where your own motivation has not matched the task, you are well on the way to understanding stress at work. Everyone has had experience of the left-hand end of the graph – being given boring work to do for no apparent purpose, or finding it difficult to get down to writing a report until the deadline is upon one. And everyone has had experience of the right-hand end, when the motivation is so strong that it interferes with the task – desperate last-minute revision for an exam, for instance, when the words don't make sense and the concepts are ungraspable; or finding that the presentation which worked well in front of one's colleagues goes to pieces in front of the Board. And just as we all recognise the role that motivation plays in our working lives, so we must all recognise that stress, resulting from the disruption of motivation, can happen to the strongest and apparently most stable people if the conditions are right for it.

Motivational problems are discussed in detail in the next chapter. Here we concentrate on the reactions people produce in stressful situations, and how these reactions can lead to poor performance.

In a stressful situation people feel threatened. Dating back from the time when we lived in caves, we have, built into our physiology, some excellent mechanisms for dealing with threat. The label given to these mechanisms is the fight/flight response. When we lived in caves, we had to work out very quickly what kind of threat faced us, and whether we stood more chance of survival if we stayed to fight, or if we ran away. On the principle of the survival of the fittest, the fight/flight mechanism got itself well ingrained into human physiology and it hasn't yet caught up with the fact that we have left the caves a long way behind. The reactions are remarkably quick. On perceiving a threat the pituitary gland sends a hormonal message throughout the body alerting it to react in fight or flight mode. Blood is withdrawn from the periphery and the gut, and goes instead to enrich the muscles. The hair stands on end, to make one appear bigger and more menacing. The pupils of the eyes dilate so as not to miss a thing. Hearing is sharpened. In short, the whole body is put on readiness to deal with the threat by either combat or flight.

This is all very well when you are living in a cave and need to be quick off the mark should a sabre-toothed tiger suddenly appear, but very inconvenient if you're at work and it's not a sabre-toothed tiger, it's the boss leaning on his buzzer saying: 'When you've got a minute, will you come and explain why you made such a mess of the new line?' No matter how much your physiology tells you to, you can't punch this threat on the nose, and you can't run away to a safer place. You have to force yourself to stay in the threatening situation while your stomach acid starts to digest your stomach wall, your startle response goes up, you breathe more shallowly, you look tense and threatened. The other people around you see your responses – consciously or unconsciously, for it's part of the same physiological situation that we notice when other members of the species have perceived a threat that we have missed. Their tension level goes up. You become panicky, reactive, defensive/aggressive, or apathetic.

We define stress as what happens when you put normal, healthy, sane people into abnormal, unhealthy, insane environments. If you're not healthy to start with – working through a cold, or back pain, or coming back to work after a bereavement – the chances of reacting badly are increased. However, to understand fully the processes of stress at work managers need to understand that while everybody's job is bound to contain some elements of stress, there are two ways of coping with that stress – the healthy way and the unhealthy way.

The *healthy* way of coping with stress includes: setting oneself reasonable objectives, not unattainable ones; changing the pace of one's work and staying in control of the pace as much as possible; keeping physically healthy and alert; and having a sense of perspective that enables one to put small incidents in their place.

The *unhealthy* way of coping with stress is to over-commit one's efforts or to withdraw completely; to redouble one's efforts when one has lost sight of one's aims; to smoke, eat or drink excessively; and to lose the sense of perspective that helps one distinguish the wood from the trees.

While in the short term the unhealthy ways of coping may, in fact, reduce the impact of the stress, over the long term they take away one's resilience and ability to tolerate additional loads.

At work, we can classify people's reactions to stress into broad fight/flight categories. 'Fight' reactions include:

quarrelsome, 'picky' behaviour
over-boisterousness
strikes and withdrawal of labour
vendettas and politicking

and 'flight' reactions include:

absenteeism
sickness (and prolonged recovery from accidents)
accidents
refusal to expand job, take initiatives, accept responsibility
reluctance to take decisions.

Nothing in life is simple; any of the above behaviours may be caused by factors other than stress. But if you see someone's behaviour suddenly change, and you think that it could be due to changes in the motivation/threat balance in his job, then perhaps he is showing signs of stress.

How managers induce stress

Here are some of the more common ways a manager can induce stress in the people working for him or her.

Giving unchallenging tasks
This may be putting people who are capable of doing more into a
situation where not much is demanded of them (e.g. assembly
line work) or putting them into situations where they need more
pressure before they work well (e.g. giving too long a deadline
or too long a planning horizon without helping the person plan
how best to use all the lead time available).

Not giving feedback
Working without knowledge of results, or with distorted knowledge of results, often causes stress. Tasks where success or
failure take years to show present particular problems for the
manager, as under these conditions people often create short-
term unimportant tasks to fill the feedback gap. Distorted feedback often happens in organisations or occupations where failure is easier to notice than success – e.g., when customers are
quick to complain about poor service but rarely write to say
thank you.

Forcing people to do a bad job
Being consistently asked to work to a standard lower than you
own is stressful. Under-manning or under-resourcing may cause
this. It also happens when senior managers or other parts of the
organisation change their minds about what they need or when
they need it. And the clash between 'perfect' and 'marketable'
causes many people to feel that they are not being asked to work
at their best.

Providing inappropriate environments
We have lost count of the number of times people have said to
us: 'The chap who designed this award-winning office should try
working here for a couple of days.'

Social ineptitude
Under this heading fall behaviours which irritate or annoy –
anything from not knowing how to run a meeting or conduct
oneself at a formal dinner through to making advances at
women co-workers.

Threat
To motivate their workforce, managers sometimes use a degree

of threat which is unacceptable and beyond what is necessary to get the job done. Making salesmen totally dependent on commission probably falls under this heading, unless the market is so good he will have no problem covering his basic living expenses. Some managers are good at using implied threats: 'Nobody goes home before I do', 'You can't go to bed until the syndicate's finished', etc.

Uncertainty
Living under uncertainty often interferes with good performance. It's difficult to concentrate if you applied for a transfer two months ago and haven't heard anything; if you've heard that your line is going to be shut down but you don't know whether the rumour is true; if lay-offs are in the air.

Pressure for spuriously clear answers
There are some situations where things are not clear, where the interactions are subtle, where for the moment the answers are: 'it depends', or 'we don't know yet', or 'the decision tree covers two sides of charting paper'. There are equally some managers who cannot tolerate the uncertainty that such situations produce and pressure their people into giving them black and white answers against their better judgement. Putting a person who is capable of subtlety and correct judgement into a situation where he is under constant pressure to be unequivocal in the teeth of the evidence causes stress.

Playing politics
Very political organisations are often stressful to work in. The essence of a political organisation is that rewards depend not on what you do but on whom you know and how well you can influence people. Some people thrive under these circumstances, but the person who believes that feedback and rewards should be based on his performance rather than on his personality and position in the network will suffer from stress.

The reader could probably add to this list from his own personal experience. Until taken to extremes what is stressful for one person may merely be fun for someone else. Many managers who induce stress in other people are probably driven by the stress they themselves are suffering. And because of the subtle link between stress and motivation it's not possible to resolve to abolish all the stress factors in a job; many of them are an intrinsic part of the job, and only stressful in excess or in inappropriate circumstances.

Neurosis and psychosis

Some form of mental illness affects one man in seven and one woman in four at some time in their lives. Psychiatrists distinguish between neurosis – where the patient knows he's ill, and psychosis – where the patient behaves abnormally (in the eyes of others) though believing himself to be normal.

Neurosis is far more common than psychosis. Many people have slight neuroses which do not get in the way of working well or enjoying oneself. There are three main kinds of neurotic behaviour:

(a) *anxiety*, where the person appears worried, concerned, jumpy, 'nervous', often without a focus for the worry;

(b) *depression*, where the person appears sad, miserable, does not notice what goes on around him, becomes inactive;

(c) *obsession*, where the sufferer has rituals – things must be arranged just so, done in a certain order or for a given number of times.

Two or three of these syndromes can combine; people become anxiety-depressive, or anxiety-obsessive, for instance. It is rare for neurosis to have a single unique cause; more likely is the combination of circumstances (heredity, early upbringing, domestic and work situations) which finally produces the neurotic behaviour. We tend to be more tolerant of some neurosis-provoking situations (e.g. bereavement, redundancy, divorce) and less tolerant of others equally powerful to the people concerned (e.g. exam nerves or interview nerves). The neurotic person knows that all is not well with him, but usually cannot find the handle to open the door for himself. The 'pull yourself together, nobody else ever reacted like this, don't be a big baby', style of advice doesn't usually help. Sympathetic listening and counselling, designed to help the sufferer work his own way out – maybe with the help of short-term psychoactive drugs – is more likely to help.

The psychotic patient is usually obviously ill to all observers except himself. Psychotic reactions include paranoia (the belief that people are plotting to damage you), delusions (the belief that things are not as they obviously are), withdrawal (isolation from the world and from human contact). While a sympathetic outsider can do a lot to help an averagely ill neurotic, a psychotic person needs professional help, probably over a long period of time.

How do you know if someone working for you is mentally ill? The following clues may help:

sudden change in behaviour from the established pattern, especially if it appears to be obviously damaging to the person
inactivity over a long period of time, or where you would expect most people to show some response
capriciousness, boisterousness, hysteria, malicious practical joking
sudden increase or decrease in the amount the person has to say
confused speech, losing track of what one's saying
extreme emotionality – or extreme lack of emotion – under circumstances that do not obviously merit this reaction
tremor and/or persistent sweating.

Change in behaviour is a much better indicator than the level of behaviour. You should always check for other reasons before suspecting mental illness, and should obviously not voice your suspicions to anyone else. As the initiative for seeking treatment must come from the person himself, all you can do is suggest that he sees his doctor and then provide a supportive atmosphere.

Alcoholism and drug abuse

Heavy drinkers are often poor performers; more likely to be late, more likely to go absent, more likely to have poor quality work, more likely to be involved in accidents. Because drinking is more socially acceptable than other drug-taking, we have much less data about the performance of people who abuse drugs, but common sense and the evidence we do have suggests that it's better not to go to work with a bloodstream awash with foreign chemicals. A particularly serious problem with alcohol

abuse is the extent to which colleagues cover up for the heavy
drinker, or even connive with him in his drinking. Being under
the influence of drink while in charge of certain items of equipment is a dismissable offence in many industries, but from time
to time the workmates whose lives have been put in jeopardy by
the drinker threaten to strike unless he is reinstated. The problem is not confined to the shopfloor; heavy regular drinking in
the management diningroom is probably as widespread and the
consequences as far-reaching.

Small amounts of alcohol do most people no harm, but a slight
deterioration in performance occurs with the first intake. Many
people feel that they perform better with some alcohol in their
blood; it's a common boast from car-driving to love-making,
from selling to writing poetry. However, as one of the first
effects of alcohol is to loosen the inhibitions and dampen the
ability to monitor one's own performance, people's actual performance starts to decline well in advance of their realising it.
Complex tasks suffer more than simple ones, and young people
are usually more affected than older ones.

How do you know if someone working for you has a drink
problem? Look for the following signs:

> *obvious signs of drink* on breath, or attempts to cover it up by
> peppermints, etc.
> *solitary* or secret drinking
> *needing a drink* before important or taxing events
> *drinking faster* than his colleagues, or drinking doubles for
> their singles
> *making excuses* for taking other people drinking
> *colleagues/subordinates* complaining that his drinking is
> affecting their work.

Other forms of drug abuse may be more difficult to identify
simply because they fall outside the experience of most managers. The regular marijuana user, for example, is difficult to spot
by any physical symptoms unless and until he becomes so
lethargic and slothful that performance deterioration is obvious;
and the regular user of small amounts of amphetamines is
equally difficult to detect. Opiate drugs such as heroin and
cocaine are so destructive, on the other hand, that their effects
show very quickly; even if the physical signs take time to appear
the money needed to support the habit may make the addict

start to steal from his workmates. People who inject opiates directly into the bloodstream develop scars and bruising; sniffing the drugs thickens the membranes of the nose, leading to a permanently runny nose, watery dilated eyes, etc. Sniffing glue – a newly popular form of abuse – produces tell-tale boils on the face, as well as signs of withdrawal and day-dreaming.

In summary: stress can happen to anyone, leading to reactions based on the fight/flight principle – reactions that can cause performance to deteriorate if they are not handled healthily. People can learn to manage their reactions to stress in a healthier fashion. Mental illness is more serious, and while laymen can help, a doctor's advice is often necessary. Drug abuse and alcoholism, similarly, need medical assistance.

How does the manager seek help in these cases? Medium to large sized companies may have a doctor in full-time employment, or a retained relationship with a local GP. A company doctor must refer an employee to his own GP for treatment and should not reveal the diagnosis to anyone else. He may advise the employee's manager about the seriousness of the illness, how the employee should be treated on his return to work, etc. The manager can help by making sure that the doctor is familiar with the circumstances the sick person has been working in. Without any direct line to a doctor or trained nurse all the individual manager can do if he suspects mental illness, alcoholism, or drug abuse, is to try to create the circumstances for a talk with the poor performer during which the manager tries to create awareness of the need for professional help.

5 Motivational problems

Most managers will be familiar – at least by reputation – with the writings of Maslow, Herzberg, and McGregor on motivation. They must forgive the brief account below, for no book on poor performance would be complete without an account of their analyses.

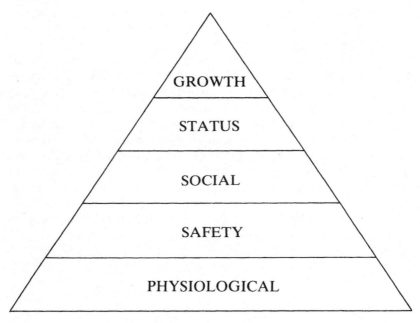

According to Maslow, human motivation, or needs, can be classified into a hierarchy. At the bottom of the hierarchy come basic physiological needs – food, water, sex, sleep, air, etc. Then come safety needs – the need to feel secure from immediate threat, the need to have a roof over one's head, etc. These are followed by social needs – needs for the companionship and friendship of other people. Next comes needs for status – feeling well-thought-of by other people. And finally come needs for self-actualisation, self-realisation, growth – the need to keep meeting new challenges and improve oneself. Maslow makes a number of points about his hierarchy:

1. Needs are satisfied from bottom to top. In other words, if there are physical needs which require attention, none of the others will matter. If the physiological needs are satisfied but there are safety needs unsatisfied, none of the higher needs will matter – the person will be driven to satisfy his safety needs first.

2. Once a need has been satisfied one ceases to be aware of it. Man does not live by bread alone – until he's hungry.

3. Needs from different parts of the hierarchy cannot be 'traded'. Someone totally lacking in friends and companionship (social needs) will not respond to offers of more luncheon vouchers, a bigger car, or a fancier-sounding title.

The consequences of this for the manager trying to understand and cure poor performance are:

1. Where someone's basic needs are threatened he will not be responsive to moves directed at another part of the hierarchy. You must find out whether the poor performer has trouble satisfying his more basic needs before investigating the higher needs. Worry about living accommodation, job security, loss of overtime, etc., will override other things.

2. People don't usually have much understanding of what motivates them, because they have become unconscious of their needs once their needs have been satisfied; and also because since Maslow's theory became widely known people think it's more socially acceptable to confess to needs at the top of the hierarchy. From time to time you may get a straight answer which shows insight into the question: 'What motivates you?' but it's unlikely.

3. Motivational needs must be addressed on their own terms, without substitution. 'We can't give you job satisfaction, but we can give you a bigger office' won't work.

4. Needs at the top of the hierarchy cannot be bargained for. You can't negotiate for people to think better of you; you can't demand that people respect you. You can get these things by your own efforts, but your union officer can't announce more of them as part of an annual settlement. This is why in an authoritarian organisation people's need to know

where they stand will not usually be satisfied by a formal participation system.

5. Needs at the bottom of the hierarchy can usually be satisfied by the expenditure of money. Needs at the top of the hierarchy are best satisfied by the expenditure of thought.

The work of Herzberg is often cited at the same time as Maslow's. Herzberg examined the conditions under which people said they worked well or felt motivated to succeed, and the conditions they said were less helpful. This led Herzberg to differentiate between two different influences on motivation: *hygiene factors* on the one hand, and *motivators* on the other. Hygiene factors are elements of the job such as the working conditions, the supervision, the bureaucracy, etc. – in fact the *context* within which the job is performed. Motivators are factors such as responsibility, recognition, challenge, and the nature of the job itself – in fact the job *content*. Herzberg said that hygiene factors and motivators affect performance at work differently, thus:

1. If the hygiene factors are wrong, work will not be done well. But once the hygiene factors are put right no amount of further effort devoted to them will improve performance; only effort devoted to increasing the motivators will then pay off.
2. Hygiene factors and motivators are not interchangeable. A need for improvement in the job context will not be met by changes in the job content, and vice versa.
3. You can spend money putting the hygiene factors right but to put the motivators to rights costs time and thought and changed behaviour.

The consequences of this for the manager trying to understand and improve poor performance are:

1. Spending money putting hygiene factors to rights will only pay off in terms of performance if the hygiene factors really need attention; and once they are right no further money will bring about improvements in performance.
2. A mickey-mouse job is a mickey-mouse job no matter whether it's done in a palace or a temporary hut, and the person who's frustrated at the mickey-mouse content of his job will not have his frustration removed by improving his accommodation or his pay.

The best commentary on Herzberg and much else comes from
Robert Townsend, who points out that the traditional forms of
'employee benefit' – social clubs, sports facilities, sick pay
schemes, pension schemes, death-in-service benefits, etc. – all
have one thing in common; you have to die or get sick or
otherwise leave the organisation in order to enjoy them.

Douglas McGregor distinguished between two theories of
human motivation which, he says, managers hold. *Theory X* says
that people dislike work, would rather not do it, need to be
coerced to perform, and need close supervision to keep them to
the job. *Theory Y* says on the other hand that people want to
work, dislike being lazy, and are capable of generating their own
interest and motivation to do the task irrespective of whether
someone is standing over them with a metaphorical lash.

McGregor also says that the theory you work to is self-
reinforcing. In other words, if you are a Theory X manager you
wil behave in such a way that people respond sullenly,
uncooperatively, and with a bad grace; thus your Theory X
perception of the world is made to come true. And if you are a
Theory Y manager you will behave in such a way that people's
natural motivation to work becomes apparent, and your theory
will be reinforced.

It is already apparent that motivation is a very complex subject; so complex that some eminent writers refuse to allow it as a
legitimate concept, or say that it is too complex to pin down. The
idea could certainly do with re-examining. But as long as managers continue to speak of motivation, and of motivation going
wrong, experts will have to translate their thoughts into these
terms. And it should be clear that however the experts differ
about the details, there *are* different needs; needs cannot be
traded for qualitatively different needs; some needs cannot be
traded for money; and people do not always have insight into
what motivates them.

So it should be obvious that poor performance is not simply a
matter of motivation being culpably low. Motivation can be
strong and frustrated – for example, the engineer who performs
badly because the production department needs the drawings
now and can't wait until they are perfect by his standards; or the
designer whose last nine projects have been cancelled because
the Board have decided to concentrate on something else.
Sometimes people have strong motivation but do not know how

to go about satisfying it – through lack of experience or good advice they have not been exposed to situations where their motivation would be used. Many women were in this position before it became accepted that they could work on their own terms; so too were children from homes and schools where career counselling was inadequate and no-one could suggest the right careers or hobbies or college subjects which the youngster should follow if he were to make best use of his interests and talents. Prolonged unemployment, too, does damage to the motivation to work; under long periods of unemployment people's time-horizons shorten, they cease to plan ahead, and they are more likely to look for short-term gratification. George Orwell wrote with sympathy and insight of the unemployed of the 1930s – when your life was drab and dull and the main reason for living had gone, you didn't sit down to budget your dole-money, or plan how you could feed the children on six-pence a week with carrots and porridge; you put the kettle on, rolled a cigarette, and sent the kids out for a pig's trotter and a packet of chips. The short-term need for stimulus and reassurance takes precedence over the longer term needs.

How do you find out what motivates your people, and whether there are things wrong with their motivation or the way their jobs satisfy their motivation? Bearing in mind how complex a subject it is, we can't offer an absolute yardstick, but we can offer a selection of questions which often give insight into people's motivation at work:

1. How satisfied are you with:
    your working conditions?
    the challenge in your job?
    how well your job uses your skills and abilities?
    your pay?
    how much time your job leaves you for social activities?
    the information you get from your manager?
    the co-operation you get from other departments?
    the level of responsibility you have in your job?
    the opportunities for training?
    the opportunities for promotion?
    the information you get about the quality of your work?
    the co-operation you get from your colleagues?

These are fairly standard attitude survey questions. If you ask them of a group of people, bear in mind that people have a tendency to agree that they are satisfied rather than grumble. We often find that where 50 per cent or less of the people say they are satisfied with one of these features, this is equivalent in morale terms to 20 per cent or more saying they are dissatisfied.

Bear in mind too that when asking people to say whether they are satisfied with their pay you must offer them at least three comparators:

(a) Are you satisfied that you are paid fairly for the amount of effort you put into your job?
(b) Are you satisfied that you are paid fairly compared with what you could get for doing a similar job in a different firm?
(c) Are you satisfied that you are paid fairly compared with what other people get in this organisation?

Of course, it's rare to find that all three of these questions elicit contented answers. But they may help you pin down the exact problem.

2. Give me examples of the following kind of events or circumstances:

events where you have felt motivated to do the best you possibly can
events where you have felt disillusioned or discouraged
routine events you like
routine events you dislike.

You should find that the answers to the above questions give you some leads on the causes of demotivation.

3. What sort of person do you have to be to do your job well? Asked in an informal interview, when people have relaxed, this question often provides startling insights into the problems they experience and the way they cope to their own satisfaction or otherwise.

4. If a friend of yours were to apply for a job here, what would you tell him? As with the previous question, a good probe in informal interviews.

5. What things stop you from doing this job to the best of your ability? Apart from being a useful investigative ques-

tion, this one has the implied supplementary 'And what can you do about it?'.

6. Have you got any skills or abilities which your present job does not use? Does your manager/supervisor/personnel officer know about them? Do you plan to do anything about this?

7. If a good fairy were to grant you a wish for something to happen at work, what would you wish for? And if the reverse were to happen and someone were to put a curse on you, what would be the worst thing that could happen?

8. How can you tell when you've done well in your job? What signs do you look for? How quickly do they become apparent? How do you tell when you've done badly? Who's the first to know?

9. How often are you prevented from doing the kind of job you would like by other people's actions?

10. All in all, would you say this is a good place to work?

If you run through these questions – and listen to the answers without imposing your own preconceptions or expectations on them – you will probably get a good deal of insight into what motivates the worker.

Try to make sense of this in Maslow's or Herzberg's terms, though you shouldn't force your data to fit their theories. You can ask whether the person is complaining about hygiene factors or motivators. Is the job context wrong? Are there some deep insecurities that prevent him looking more widely and taking initiatives? What are his expectations about how he is supposed to behave at work and be managed? Could you achieve a change in behaviour if you changed some of these expectations?

People rarely suffer from all-round low motivation. The sullen youth who slouches over his machine goes home to work with loving care on rebuilding an old car; the gossipy secretary examining her nails by the typewriter spends hours learning new dance steps; the manager who never uses his initiative and never makes a suggestion works on his golf swing as if his life depended on it. Your problem as a manager is to discover why he or she thinks that work is not the right environment for high standards and devotion, and then try to work towards the necessary changes.

6 Medical disorders

It is possible that your poor performer's difficulties are caused by a medical condition. Of the innumerable medical conditions which affect people's behaviour, we shall concentrate here on some of the more common ones from which people may suffer *while staying in work*, and the management these conditions require. Someone with diabetes or epilepsy or a slipped disc does not automatically need to retire from work; he can carry on, with a few adjustments to his lifestyle. Unfortunately sometimes the adjustments fail, or the person is not willing to let it be known that he suffers from a medical condition. Then people may think he has lost his will to work, or is reluctant to take on new responsibilities, though a little more understanding and help could overcome the problem.

Diabetes

This is caused by a malfunction in the way the body processes sugar. Diabetics do not produce enough of the right substance – insulin – and have to supplement their body's production of insulin by regular injections. In the non-diabetic insulin is produced as it is needed, depending on the amount of sugar to be dealt with. The diabetic does not have this fine internal balance; and because he injects fixed amounts of insulin, things are more likely to go wrong. If a diabetic is forced to go without food the over-supply of insulin in the bloodstream produces faintness, pallor, a feeling of malaise, and in severe cases unconsciousness and death. Many diabetics have learned to recognise the signs of possible insulin coma, and they carry sugar lumps in their pocket for use in emergency. A diabetic should not be asked to endure situations where he must go for a long time without a meal, or (in some cases) where he does not have control over his mealtimes. The negotiating situation where you must show your machismo by sitting round the table for fourteen hours without a break is a difficult one for most diabetics. Apart from this one proviso about the importance of controlling their food intake there is no

53

reason why a diabetic should automatically be unsuitable for particular kinds of work.

Epilepsy

This exists in two forms –*petit mal* and *grand mal* (literally, small illness and large illness). No-one is really sure what causes epilepsy; it is a malfunction in the brain, it often disappears or improves after adolescence, and with modern drugs can be kept largely or completely under control. *Petit mal* usually shows itself in short blackouts, maybe lasting only a couple of seconds. The person suffering them may say: 'I was just walking down the corridor and when I got to the end I realised I didn't know how I had got there.' To the outside observer this episode might have appeared as if the sufferer was momentarily not 'with it' and his eyes glazed over. Sufferers from *petit mal* are often advised not to drive or operate machinery because of the problems these minor blackouts can cause. In recognition of the way the disease can be controlled through the use of drugs and its tendency to disappear with age, this rule is often relaxed and the person need demonstrate only that he has gone for a given number of years without an episode.

   Grand mal is, as its name implies, more serious – but it is still controllable. Untreated, it produces the classic 'fits' beloved of writers of lurid fiction. Treated with modern drugs it can often be suppressed until it becomes comparable with *petit mal* in its effects. There are certain circumstances where an episode can be triggered by exposure to regular rapid flashes of light – under the rotating blades of a helicopter, in a disco, driving along the motorway at night with fast regularly spaced traffic coming in the opposite direction, defective fluorescent tube lighting. It is important to remember that epileptics are not necessarily different in other respects from the rest of the population; they are not less intelligent, more introverted, or more neurotic.

Migraine

This is a violent headache which affects half the head (hence the name, *hemi-crania*) and may be accompanied by feeling of nausea, seeing flashing lights, losing part of the visual field, and other nasty symptoms. In some people migraine attacks are brought on by eating certain foods (chocolate and alcohol are often mentioned as culprits). In others migraine is brought on by over-sleeping, or occurs after a time of tension is over – Saturday morning is a common time for migraines. Treatment is often a matter of trial and error. There are drugs which can help if taken at the right time, which is often at the very beginning of an attack. Sometimes with a really bad migraine there is no alternative to lying down in a dark room until it's all over. If you have a migraine sufferer working for you who believes that the only thing to do is to double up on the aspirin and keep at it, it's worth encouraging them to go back to the doctor to see if some of the newer drugs will help suppress the problem. And do take the pain seriously – several people have killed themselves rather than face a life of regular migraines.

Varicose veins, etc.

The 'etc.' means piles. They are one of the disadvantages of being an upright animal. We stand up, so putting strain on our back muscles and the blood supply to the legs; and we eat a low-residue diet leading to constipation and what Pepys called 'straining at stool'. Eventually the strained and damaged veins lose their elasticity and become distended, painful, and sometimes infected. Unfortunately, in the present state of the National Health Service in Britain they are the kind of non-life-threatening, boring (for the doctors) problems which get pushed to the end of the waiting list. For people thus afflicted, unrelieved standing about, particularly without an opportunity to change position, or sitting on uncomfortable chairs can be acutely painful. Varicose veins are likely to bleed with frightening profusion if damaged – bleeding which stops if the person lies down with his legs up – and this may make him overprotective if he's had one scaring episode. People are often reluctant to mention that they suffer from piles or varicose veins, and they can ask themselves to do ridiculous things rather than admit publicly what the problem is.

Slipped discs and other back problems

'A bad back' is too often the malingerer's favourite complaint; turn up at the surgery on a busy Monday morning complaining

of pains in the lower back and there's not much the GP can do to
disprove it even if he feels so inclined. This makes things difficult
for the people with genuine back problems – slipped discs,
strained muscles, etc. And for these genuine cases medicine may
not have help available; often all that can be offered is an
alleviation of the symptoms.

Standing or sitting for long periods in the same position causes
discomfort to back sufferers. They need opportunities to move
about and stop themselves 'locking'. The 'orthopaedic' chairs
sometimes advertised need looking at with care; what may seem
to the layman to be most suitable for someone with a back
problem could in fact do harm. If you care for your back sufferer
enough to want to get him a special chair do get advice from a
doctor first. And make sure that *everyone* knows how to lift a
bulky heavy object. Plenty of factories have safety notices telling the people on the shopfloor how to lift something, but one
rarely sees these notices in offices where people manhandle
typewriters, desks, heavy parcels, etc.

Pre-menstrual tension

It is generally accepted that women tend to be more vulnerable
during the few days preceding their monthly periods. Studies
have shown that a wide variety of unpleasant things, ranging
from shoplifting to traffic accidents, and many minor illnesses,
are more common in the pre-menstrual period. It is furthermore
well established by doctors – though not so well accepted elsewhere – that any woman can experience pre-menstrual tension.
It's not just the neurotic who suffer; nor will getting married and
having a baby bring automatic relief. There are two kinds of
'period pains' – the spasmodic and the congestive varieties.
Women tend to get either one or the other, not both. The
spasmodic pain is experienced as sharp cramping pains in the
abdomen, coming on as the period starts, often relieved by a hot
water bottle. Congestive pains, on the other hand, happen in the
few days before the period starts; they are experienced as feelings of lassitude, heaviness, backache, and 'dragging' pains,
usually disappearing when the period starts. These two different
kinds of period pain are associated with two possible kinds of
hormone imbalance, needing different kinds of treatment.
However, you should not expect women workers to need a

couple of days off every month as a matter of routine. In the last few years doctors have become much more skilled at treating pre-menstrual symptoms, and menopausal symptoms, and it should be rare for performance at work to suffer as a result of this problem.

With many medical problems prevention is better than cure, and organisations can take initiatives which are not always open to individuals. Health insurance, safety training, smoking clinics, gymnasiums, etc., may be more easily available at work than outside. But there is one further unresolved problem area that the individual manager faces when one of his people reports that he has a medical problem; put crudely, it is: 'How do I know he isn't swinging the lead?'

The present state of affairs in the UK at the moment is not helpful. No doctor can refuse to sign a sick note if the patient presses him. The doctor's relationship is with his patient, not with the patient's employer. The doctor has no obligation to disclose information to the patient's employer, even if the patient is being obviously dishonest. This means that the truth-fulness of the sick note is left in the hands of the individual doctor, and it depends on his attitudes, his knowledge of local conditions, and the pressure he works under, whether he gives in to the patient's demands or puts up a fight. At one end of the spectrum you will find doctors who leave a pile of signed sick notes with the receptionist ready for the patient to write in his own diagnosis; we know one firm where a factory closure was accelerated by the way the local doctor contributed to an absen-teeism rate greater than 20 per cent. At the other end are doctors who resist giving free sick notes and if the patient presses writes: 'I have examined Mr X and he says he is suffering from . . .' However, the individual employer has no way legally of discovering whether someone's absence is genuinely medical, unless he brings in the big guns. The big guns are the clauses written into many contracts of employment stipulating that after an absence of x weeks the employee shall be examined by the firm's own doctor. If you have these clauses you can usually discover the serious malingerers, but there is no course of action in between; either you believe what the employee's doctor tells you, or you summon the employee before a doctor of your own choosing. This can lead to poor morale, and it doesn't help if your employee takes short breaks of two or three days. The introduction of self-certification for short sicknesses has made this position worse in some firms, as has the growth in expectation that a worker is allowed so many days' statutory sick leave, which he takes whether he is ill or no. This abuse is a sign of a more fundamental malaise, for it tends not to happen in organisations where there is a high degree of trust, and is rife where industrial relations are poor. The long-term answer is to work on the absence of trust, but this is a commodity difficult to restore once it has been lost. In the short term, the solution is probably much more reliance on the firm's own doctor, *plus* a very clearly defined policy, applied by all managers, so that people know there are severe and invariant penalties for telling lies. The individual manager is left to find out what he can by individual questioning of the employee, or – and don't discount this – peer group pressure if his persistent absenteeism causes the performance of the whole team to deteriorate. If the rest of the team, or the local union representative, is on your side, you may find that they detect the malingerer and take action more easily than you can from your position of authority.

The position in the UK is open to a good deal of abuse. Large firms with access to their own doctor are better off than smaller ones. It's worth taking a corporate initiative and holding an open evening where local doctors can come and see the circumstances their patients work in, and incidentally learn something about the problems the profligate use of sick notes causes the employer.

7 Work groups

Most managers, asked to give examples of how the work group can turn someone into an unsatisfactory performer, would cite strikes and other forms of industrial action as prime instances. And whenever there is a national strike or major dispute, it seems that the media can always unearth at least one person to say: 'Well, if it was up to me I wouldn't strike, but if the rest of the lads walk out then I'm bound to follow them.' In fact the issues are more subtle than is commonly made out in times of crisis, but there is no doubt that the worker's feelings about the rest of the people he works with can affect the quality and quantity of the work he does.

Very few people prefer to work totally without social contact. There are some occupations that seem solitary – light-housekeepers, authors, out-workers, but even these people need regular relief or the approval of their peers if they are to continue. A musician like Havergal Brian, writing without hope of publication, performance, or academic approval for most of his long life, is a very rare exception. For most people, starting work means joining a group of strangers – strangers with whom they will spend most of their working time, under their influence much more than their managers' or supervisors' control. Getting on with this group of strangers demands some effort, especially for the first job, where the newcomer will probably be working alongside people from a wider background of age and experience than he has ever associated with before. The effort involved in learning to be accepted by this new group means that the group's approval comes to be valued for its own sake.

This fact is generally recognised by people who try to change attitudes at work. Peer group pressure is probably the single best method of getting someone to change his attitude and have it stay changed. Peer group pressure takes time to work, and needs careful management, but the peer group can accomplish changes where training, discipline, reward, and rational persuasion have all failed.

What are the implications of this for understanding poor

performance? There are two common causes of poor performance associated with the work group:

Norms and output limitation

It is a common observation that in a group of people who are all
working at the same task output tends to remain fairly constant
between workers. By a process more or less overt the group
produces its own norms about how much it should produce.
People who consistently produce more than the rest of the group
are given a warning. This anecdote about starting work in a
corset factory shows how 'rate-busters' are dealt with:

> They began by putting me at the learners' table. That's where
> you sit with the other youngsters assembling small parts like
> suspenders or straps and bundling them up into dozens for the
> out-workers. I could do it quite fast, and soon the pile in the
> trough in front of me was bigger than the others. The other
> girls started making pointed remarks about this, to the effect
> that I would soon be doing them all out of a job. We were on
> an hourly rate, not piecework, but they didn't seem at all
> happy that I should be working faster than them. Then they
> started to point out small faults in the work, implying that it
> was better to go slow but not make any mistakes. This even
> went so far as to require me to tie my bundles differently, even
> though they only went up to the other end of the room before
> they were untied again. You got the impression that sewing
> suspenders onto bias tape was a craft of a high order. Then I
> got put onto piece-work, with my own machine for making
> parts of the corsets. If you looked down the workroom you'd
> see the women on piece-work seemed to have their heads
> down all the time, running up one seam and down the next
> without looking up. All the stuff they needed was put near
> them so they wouldn't have to break rhythm by reaching, and
> if they did want anything they would call for one of the
> learners to get it. But actually when you got to be one of them
> you found out that they each knew practically to the penny
> what they had made that day, and what everyone else had
> made too, and there were fairly strict limits either side of that
> amount. If your work slowed up – particularly if it went on to
> someone else for additional work – people would barrack
> you, or help you, and in extreme circumstances they would all

work through their break to help you catch úp. But if you went too fast you'd get the sarcastic comments to begin with, and then someone would have a quiet word with you to the effect that if you continued to go at that speed management would just re-time the job and everyone would be worse off. There was no way you could argue – all the older women seemed to club together and have their different ways of telling you to slow down.

There *were* times when it was accepted that you could put a bit of a spurt on without spoiling things – just before the annual holiday people stopped taking the unofficial breaks, everyone really buckled down, and wage packets were up 30 per cent. And if one of the women were leaving to have a baby she'd be allowed to work as hard as she could while there was still the chance of two incomes coming in. I suppose that Christmas would have been a similar time; but apart from that it was a mostly wordless conspiracy to keep earnings regular and stable.

When groups have an output norm, it usually has a lower boundary as well as an upper one, especially if the groups are interdependent; very slack performers are seen as a threat just as much as rate-busters. The same mechanism is at work in the phenomenon of 'self-compensating absenteeism' seen in some heavy manual industries; here there appears to be an unwritten agreement between the workers that a particularly hard shift merits some time off in lieu, but the amount of time taken is regulated according to an (often unverbalised) code, and any-one who gets greedy and takes more than he deserves soon finds out about it. Fiddling from the till often obeys the same rules; a certain amount is tolerated, but you mustn't get greedy. Often the local supervisor connives by not reporting abuses within the permitted level.

Group restrictions on output are easiest to observe in manual work, and on piece-rates. Similar pressures apply in many other jobs. Children who try too hard at school may be called Swot and Teacher's Pet. Work through your lunch hours and sooner or later colleagues will pass comments not wholly expressive of a disinterested concern for your health. Suggest that to save time you substitute a conference telephone call for a meeting and you'll find people referring to you as 'our efficiency watchdog'. Note the number of students who, finding that they can't settle down to work themselves, come and disrupt someone else's studies.

The key to understanding these group norms is to see them as a psychologically sensible price which the worker pays in order to be accepted as a member of a group which he values. They are not necessarily a symptom of bloody-mindedness or dislike of management, though they may turn into these if relations at the workplace become too sour. The consequences for the manager are:

1. If you put a fast worker into a slow group in the hope that he will set them an example, the stratagem will probably fail unless you can make it rewarding for the group to follow him. Otherwise the group influence on him will be stronger than his influence on the group.

2. If you want to improve the performance of a single poor performer by putting him into a high-performing group, make the gap between his performance and theirs big enough to be obvious, but not so big as to be daunting.

3. If you want to improve the performance of the whole group you must make the changed performance attractive to the whole group, while leaving them with the feeling that they are in control of some aspects of the work.

Remember that logic doesn't change behaviour; people are motivated by things other than money alone; and that as a manager you have much less daily influence on people than do their mates.

Rejection by the work group

Once upon a time the expression 'sent to Coventry' was widely used to describe a situation where someone's workmates had stopped talking to him. You don't hear the phrase so often nowadays, but the practice remains. People transgress the norms of the work group and the group responds by excluding them. It is rare for this not to have a damaging effect on performance.

The most common candidate for rejection is the person who has somehow set himself aside as different from the rest of the group. Just the fact of being different – hence unfamiliar, hence more difficult to predict, hence threatening – will do. Among the most common instances of people being rejected for their differences from the rest of the group are:

(a) the worker who refuses to join a strike or go-slow because it does not agree with his own value system;
(b) the worker who is more educated than the rest of the work group, having been to college or to grammar school;
(c) the worker with considerably less education than the rest of the group, or with education objectively as good but obtained from a disapproved establishment;
(d) the worker who has a different regional accent from the rest of the group, especially where the accent implies social standing;
(e) the worker of a different race or nationality or colour from the rest of the group – or in some areas the worker of a different religion;
(f) the worker of a different age from the rest of the group;
(g) the foreman or supervisor who had been promoted from inside the work group and now has to supervise the people who were until recently his mates – usually neither he nor they know what to expect.

Rejection shows itself in a number of ways. The possibility of group rejection is seen in many of the 'initiation ceremonies' which newcomers have to go through; American colleges, the military everywhere, and many workplaces, are notorious for having often savage initiation rites where the newcomer must undergo humiliation and/or physical pain. It's a lucky youngster who finds that the most he has to do is go for a bucket of steam, or a long weight; the more intimate initiation rites are well documented by hospital casualty wards. White-collar groups have their own rites too; heavy drinking sessions, visits to strip clubs, etc. In very formal groups the entrance gestures are made overt and formalised; in less formal groups the entrance rituals are less open, but people know well who is 'one of us' and who isn't.

Groups demand certain standards of behaviour from their members. If someone's standards slip, he may be out. Groups usually do not demand that everyone behave the same; look at any established group and you will see different behaviour patterns from different people. One or two people are generally recognised as leaders; they set standards, give directions, and

are listened to and respected by most members. Most groups
have a joker or buffoon; many have someone who is allowed to
break some of the rules because the members like the feeling
they get when they tolerate his eccentricities. Many groups have
a housekeeper/pedant – someone who keeps track of everything, worries when things aren't going to plan, counts that
everyone is here, and makes lists of what everyone wants.
Within each group different roles are performed by different
people, but the group as a whole has certain common standards
and it understands who has which role. When someone starts to
behave out of role, or to behave to different standards, the
group starts to suspect him and the rejection process begins.

Sometimes rejection starts with the social side of the job; the
group stops asking the outcast to join them for mealbreaks, or
they leave him out of the visits to the pub on the way home.
No-one offers to get him a cup of coffee when they're collecting
group orders. No-one tells him the latest gossip, shows him the
juicy bits in the papers, asks how his family is. Or the rejection
starts with the job itself. People have had their work sabotaged,
their tools spoilt, their clothes ruined. The captain of the Trident
aircraft Papa India had to look at insulting graffiti about himself on the ground and in his cockpit before suffering a heart
attack and crashing the plane – graffiti written by his intelligent,
educated, highly-paid co-workers because he had not supported
the notion of a pilots' strike. Most of the instances of rejection at
work do not have such disastrous effects; instead the outcast
never hears about the good opportunities for overtime, gets the
difficult patch to work, finds himself with the oldest machine or
the worst customers or the most difficult product.

It is a rare person who can tolerate this amount of rejection
and still work well. Work suffers because the person puts more
effort into winning back the esteem of the work group, at the
expense of what management want him to do. Or he expends
time and effort involving outsiders – union officers, legal representatives, etc. – to get the ostracism called off; and while
pressure from statutory bodies may help you get the job if you're
a member of a minority group, no amount of legislation will
make people want to ask you to join them for lunch. Probably
the single group suffering most from rejection are the people
who are made supervisors or foremen after some years working
alongside those whom they now have to supervise. Figures on

the incidence of stress-related diseases show that this group is probably more liable to early death linked to stress than any other group in British industry. (Analysis of stress at work is complicated by the need to take into account both the incidence of stress and the healthiness of the person's reaction to stress; in the late-promoted supervisor we probably have a combination of both factors at work.) Any supervisor put into this position – especially if he has to work as well as supervise – needs special training and guidance on how to conduct himself in this difficult position.

It's worth trying to look at your own organisation to see how much peer group pressure is used as a motivator, because then you'll have some idea of how poor performance can be induced by these pressures when they take different direction from management's ideal. Do you have a '100 per cent club' for salesmen who reach their targets, together with the ballyhoo and special ties and applause at the annual conference? Do you have graduate association dinners? Course reunions? Branch proficiency competitions? We are not saying that these are a bad thing; they can be excellent motivators in the right hands, but if you are the kind of organisation where peer group pressures are used a lot then you should be more prepared for the consequences should pressures go wrong. Over-attachment, or rejection, can be equally damaging to performance.

8 The organisation

The organisation itself can induce poor performance in a variety of ways. People who in other circumstances would do well may not do a good job in your firm because of actions taken elsewhere in the organisation, or because of the organisation's structure. This chapter describes the most common ways in which organisations contribute to poor performance.

Tolerance of poor standards

Managers sometimes refuse to take corrective action when they see someone performing badly. It might be too much trouble; it might prejudice a negotiation going elsewhere; the person may be coming up for retirement and therefore not seem worth the effort; the person may be new and therefore need time to settle down; the manager may not know how to start; he may have other things to do; and in any case it's embarrassing to talk to another adult about his performance. If the manager can distance himself from the problem – most commonly by blaming it on outside causes or a poor recruitment decision – the abdication feels even more comfortable.

Individual managers use all these excuses, and more, for not getting to grips with poor performers. In many organisations they can be excused because the policy decisions and the necessary training do not exist. It is rare for an organisation to have a well-thought-out policy about what to do with poor performers; most now have a policy for *dismissals,* but we are interested here in methods of pulling people back from that brink. Managers often complain that their actions about poor performers are reversed on appeal to a higher authority, or because of union pressure. It is rare to find an organisation prepared to train managers to deal with poor performers, and when the issue arises on training courses the trainers usually duck it.

Though the best person to correct small failings is the supervisor or foreman, they are in our experience unlikely to see this as their responsibility. It's a particular problem when the supervisor works alongside the team, with supervisory responsibilities added on; and it's made worse if the supervisor is not involved in the selection decision. We have worked with groups of supervisors trying to develop the skills of correcting poor performance, and there is always an enormous obstacle to be overcome first as the supervisors refuse to see it as their problem – after all, if they didn't cause the problem, why should they admit responsibility for correcting it?

As long as people see poor standards being tolerated, or the subject of bargaining, they will see no need to try to improve their own performance. The same argument holds in reverse – as long as people see that good performance goes unnoticed and unpraised, they will see no point in trying hard. Eventually the poor standards become endemic; the good workers, who want to do well, leave; and all that remains is a group of dispirited people who knew they couldn't get a job elsewhere if they wanted one.

Poor induction

If you plot a graph of the number of people leaving your organisation against their length of service you will probably find one or two large bumps in the curve, representing people leaving in relatively large numbers after only a short time with you. The size of this bump, multiplied by what it costs to recruit and train and manage these people, is one measure of the costs of poor induction training. Another measure is the amount of poor performance that can be assigned to poor induction training, as people struggle to grasp the essentials of their job without training or guidance. If you have a recently-recruited person working for you whose performance is not all you could wish it is worth checking whether they have had proper induction training. Induction training should include the following, at least:

(a) what the firm does for a living – its products, its customers, its suppliers;
(b) how the newcomer's department fits into the organisation structure;
(c) where the work done in his department comes from and goes to;
(d) company geography, acronyms, local slang;
(e) the skills the newcomer will need to use;

(f) the degree of discretion he will have in planning his work;

(g) the company 'etiquette' so that he does not unwittingly offend someone, or spend without authority;

(h) whom he can ask if he has any questions at all in his settling-down process.

Induction training, for most people, needs to happen in two stages. At first people need basic information including the points listed above. But there must be a later stage, after they have settled down a little and met some people, where the information about what the firm does and how their work will contribute gets repeated in more detail. With an unskilled manual worker the induction process may be over in hours or days; with a graduate entrant the process could take months. The knowledge worker needs a different kind of induction from the manual worker; the knowledge worker coming into a new company probably knows the basics of what the company wants him to do, but in the early stages lacks the contextual information necessary to plan the work. The manual worker has his work largely planned for him. The knowledge worker – especially the new one – knows what to do, and his frustration may arise from his inability to plan and organise his own work so that it fits in properly. Younger knowledge workers usually don't recognise that this is the crisis, and grumble that their skills are being unused. Older knowledge workers are more likely to anticipate this crisis and take action on their own initiative.

Selection errors

Your poor performer could be doing badly because he has not been properly selected. Most selection processes could benefit from some concentrated research to find out what they should be looking for and how they should look for it. If your personnel departments are relying on the unstructured interview for making appointments – and most of them still are – then you are having more poor performers than necessary thrust upon you through no fault of yours or theirs. In your selection procedures, do you have a clear idea of the skills and abilities you are looking for, and how they relate to the job to be done? Are qualifications checked and references taken up? Does the selection interview follow a systematic plan? If there is more than one interviewer, are responsibilities clearly assigned between them?

Is the selection interview supplemented where necessary by reliable tests of ability or personality? Is the selection interview supplemented where necessary by properly organised and observed group selection? If you make the selections yourself, have you have been trained to do this? As a line manager, have you ever been asked to communicate your standards to the personnel experts charged with finding people for you? Do you know your own biases and weaknesses as a selector?

If the answer to most of these questions is *No,* or *I don't know,* then there's a fair chance that some poor performers are working for your organisation because they should never have been hired. And while this is not the book for a discussion of how to improve your selection methods, here are one or two ways for you to detect whether you may be the victim of a hiring error so that you can try to avoid the mistake next time:

1. Did the performance start bad and get worse?
2. Does he say that the job is very different from what he thought it would be?
3. Does he say that there are important parts of the job which he doubts he will ever be able to learn?
4. Does the person who selected him confess to having had doubts about his suitability?
5. What does he say if you offer him the chance of leaving or starting again in a different department with no hard feelings or adverse records?

Inadequate performance appraisal

He may not actually know he's a poor performer unless you have communicated to him the standards he's supposed to work to. All managers should do this as a regular routine. In addition to the regular informal communication of work content and standards many organisations have performance appraisal systems where the person's performance is reviewed over the past year and planned for the coming year. It's not uncommon for consultants to ask someone: 'What do you see as the main purpose of your job? and to ask his manager: 'What do you see as the main purpose of his job?' and get two contradictory answers that can never be explained by reference to differences in level or perspective. The worker really must know what is expected of him before he can be judged, and performance appraisal systems

provide one method of ensuring that standards are communicated at least annually.

There are many ways for managers to neglect these duties. If
you leave all communication about standards until the annual
performance appraisal you have the opportunity for eleven
months' slippage between discussions. If someone is doing badly
– or doing well, or doing moderately – he should not have to wait
until the annual appraisal to know this. Another way for managers to shirk their responsibilities is to avoid giving a poor rating
because they don't want the unpleasantness involved in defend-
ing it. It's easier to book the appraisal interview for 4.30 p.m. on
a Friday and hope to get away with a C rating. Organisations
connive at these deceptive practices if they load the appraisal
system so that promotability is judged according to present
rating of potential; if this happens without sensitive checking,
the chances are that some managers will puff their poor performers – to get rid of them onto some other sucker – and give
poorer grades to the workers who are actually keeping the place
going. There is at least one large UK firm where the appraisal
system has become so corrupted by these practices that nothing
good can come of it or any other performance review system.

If you suspect that your poor performer does not know what
standards he is supposed to work to – maybe you have just taken
over a department and think you have some dubious legacies –
try asking the following questions:

1. Does he know what he is supposed to be doing? What
   does he see as the main tasks and responsibilities of his
   present job?
2. Does he know what standards he is supposed to work to?
   Can he give you examples of what would be poor work,
   acceptable work, and excellent work, in his job?
3. What is his estimate of his current performance, and on
   what evidence does he base that assessment?
4. When was the last time he knew for certain that his
   performance had been assessed; what was that assessment; and did he think it had been fairly arrived at?

Ageing organisations

Old organisations often have a particular pattern of poor performance, easier for the outsider to spot than for people who

have grown up there. In old organisations several factors may combine to produce poor performance. One factor is the average length of service of employees, making it difficult for them to react to change, and resistant to attempts to change them. Another is the average length of stay in the same job. In old organisations the novelty has often worn off a long time ago. Yet another is that old organisations have a weight of tradition, internal and external, weighing them down; neither employees nor customers expect them to change. And in these organisations you will often find people who have been doing the job for ten years, having been taught it by someone who did it for fifteen years, who had been taught it by someone who had done it for twelve years . . . until you find that the original job began at about the turn of the century and any notion of the 'mission' of the job has long since gone; instead the people come to think of the job as a series of operations they perform on data or material with no thought of the end user.

In ageing organisations tradition becomes a pre-conscious habit, so that people censor new ideas before they're aware of having had them. Where there is a structure which appears inviolate – a railway system, a reporting structure, a command structure – people get more efficient at getting more out of the system, but take the system itself for granted. And in old organisations you very often find the kind of management structure that makes it very difficult for an individual manager to take action to improve poor performance; for instance, in some of the old insurance companies there is a grade structure such that any Grade 4 in a branch office can tell any Grade 5 in the same department what to do, without the Grade 5 having a manager he can call his own. Poor performers get dealt with formally by the personnel department when things get bad, but it's no-one's task to try to prevent below average performance from getting worse.

Many ageing organisations are also poor, have out-of-date working conditions, are in locations no longer favoured. The individual manager may find his own standards dragged down; he may find poor performance difficult to pinpoint against this rather mediocre background. We do not mean to say that therefore old organisations should lie down quietly and die; it is possible for them to pick themselves up and show the rest of us a clean pair of heels. What managers in old organisations seem to us to lack most of all is contact with other managers who might give them a different perspective on performance standards and methods for improvement.

Inappropriate spans of control

Organisations contribute to poor performance if they give a manager too many people to be responsible for. There's no hard and fast rule here, but much above ten and you're probably in trouble, and in some organisations the number should be smaller. We have met managers who have forty performance appraisals to do in January. They just can't do them without insulting the people they are supposed to benefit. Can people see you if they really need to, without your having to juggle a dozen other appointments? Do you get the chance to see or talk to your people at least once a week? If not, maybe you are looking after too many people and need to put in an additional level of day-to-day supervision. Inappropriate spans of control may result in people being badly prepared for their next promotion. This is a common finding in national retail chains. Here the branch manager is often recruited locally, having risen from the sales staff, and in most cases his function is supervisory. Branch managers are looked after by a district manager, who spends most of his time on the road driving between branches; once they get to a branch their functions are largely control, discipline, and checking. District managers report in to a head office, where the marketing and forward planning decisions are made. In response to centralised buying to cut costs, and centralised management because retailing, at least in some countries, typically attracts poor quality staff, the disparity in function between a branch manager and a district manager becomes so great that success as a branch manager is no predictor of success as a district manager. The difference in function at different levels combines with the problems of geography to make the development of good managers very difficult.

Poor training

Some people benefit from training; some are unscathed; and some come back worse than they went. Training can turn someone into a poor performer in a variety of interesting ways.

The simplest way in which training can produce poor performers is by training to different standards from the ones in use in the organisation. If the course uses Imperial measures and you're on metric, or teaches academic French when you want business French, or teaches financial control in a manufacturing plant when you actually run a charity – you've wasted the money and time spent on training, and have lost the esteem of the trainee. A significant part of the British Civil Service uses an external course on report-writing which recommends the use of the first person, putting the conclusions and recommendations first, etc., in the teeth of the evidence that standard Civil Service practice is exactly the opposite. Millions of pounds have had to be spent training salesmen to close the sale and handle objections, largely because earlier training had put undue emphasis on eliciting objections.

Training can use the wrong method; we see this with T-groups and sensitivity training sessions, and their later progeny, where people are asked to confront their own personal style and the impact they have on other people. If these sessions are run in a self-indulgent way a trainee with a high need for structure may suffer temporary or permanent damage. Fortunately this does not happen often; more frequently one encounters a trainer whose lack of flexibility makes it difficult for him to make his trainees feel comfortable and confident.

The worst way in which an organisation can generate poor performers amongst trainees is by not supporting the training when they get back into the field. Trying a new way of doing anything – holding your golf club, playing consecutive sixths, typing, negotiating – nearly always results in a short-term decline in performance as the new style takes a while to settle down. It is easy for the trainee or his manager to look at the new level of performance and say: 'That course has made you worse; better go back to the tried and tested way of doing things.' Concentrating on short-term results rather than on behaviour makes this even more likely to happen; so the trainee gives up his new and potentially more fruitful way of doing things, and reverts to his old ways. Training needs field support; it needs managers who will help the trainee over the 'results dip' until the rewards of the new skills start to come in and reinforce the training.

In selecting these examples of ways in which an organisation can actually promote poor performance we have chosen only a sample. As a final check-list, here are some things to look for if you wonder whether your organisation encourages or shelters poor performers:

1. Do we have many people leaving us who we think badly of but do very well in their next jobs?
2. Do we have more trouble than other comparable firms filling vacancies and keeping them filled?
3. Do we seem to spend a lot of time on internal political squabbles?
4. Do people say No rather than Yes to most new ideas?
5. Do I personally know what my responsibilities are and what I have to do to achieve them?
6. Do I personally know how I stand with my own manager?

9 Working conditions

In Chapter 5 we discussed the difference between motivators and hygiene factors, and referred to Maslow's hierarchy of needs; these two concepts lead to the conclusion that if working conditions are inappropriate good performance will be inhibited, though the difference between acceptable working conditions and superb working conditions may not have much direct effect on performance.

Maslow, Herzberg, and their followers were inclined to state these findings as if they were universal truths, ignoring the fact that their research was conducted mainly on white American east-coast males. With experience, many people have found that these findings are not universal. If you are making a new exciting product the chances are you'll spend all the hours God sends working in a draughty garage or lock-up in the most primitive of working conditions, and later on when you've made your million and sold out to Lonrho you'll look back on those days with the fondest nostalgia. Even when people are no longer in the pioneering stage there are some jobs, and some organisations where physical working conditions are not good, but people accept them; in British Rail, for instance, most people say: 'If you come to work for the railway you don't expect potted palms and fitted carpets; if you get them it's a nice bonus, but nobody complains if they have to get wet and dirty and work nights sometimes.'

Having acknowledged these cautions against uncritical acceptance of the findings of Maslow and Herzberg, we must also admit that there are many circumstances where inappropriate working conditions contribute to poor performance. Some of the main problems are:

Temperature and humidity

For most people a temperature above 80°F is difficult to work in, especially if the humidity is high. Prolonged exposure to temperatures in the high nineties and above leads to heat stroke and death if medical attention is not received quickly. Low temperatures may cause hypothermia, although it is not possible to be exact about temperatures here because much depends on the amount of clothing worn and the degree of activity. Statutory regulations on safety and health at work usually limit the degree to which people are exposed to these perils, but they should be borne in mind if freak weather conditions occur or the worker has to go to a country where he will be exposed to extremes of temperature.

Less well regulated, but possibly more harmful, is humidity – the moisture content of the air. Humid atmospheres are difficult to work in. Very dry atmospheres are less difficult, apart from chapped lips and electric shocks from the carpet. Much of the difficulty – lethargy, headaches, sleepiness – caused by too high humidity can be alleviated by changing the ion balance of the air; in a humid atmosphere the air is overloaded with positive ions (charged particles) while experiments have shown that people perform better and feel better when the atmosphere is over-supplied with negative ions. However at the time of writing no-one has managed to produce a commercial air ioniser which produces a cheap effective source of negative ions in a quantity useful for the office or factory.

Noise

Noise is one of those things – like elephants, leadership, and being in love – which people cannot define but can surely recognise when they experience it. Noise interferes with performance in a variety of ways. Very loud noise disrupts concentration in the short term and prolonged exposure leads to permanent hearing loss. But noise does not have to be painfully loud to interfere with performance; if it is unpredictably intermittent, or of a quality that one does not like, even a low noise can be disruptive.

It is also possible for working conditions to be too quiet for people to work well. There is a story of a cigarette lighter factory where the management, concerned that they had a noisy production process whose assembly line characteristics did not fit modern management theories, re-designed the factory so that small teams of workers worked in carpeted areas with screens to ensure privacy. The expected improvements in productivity did

not materialise, so a psychologist was called in. He observed that
– amongst other things – the workers took care to walk on the
uncarpeted bits of floor. In following up this clue he learned that
the work force felt that the place was 'too quiet,' 'eerie,' 'didn't
feel like a proper place to work', etc. He recommended a
number of changes which included increasing the background
noise a bit, and production and morale improved. The same
considerations were applied to the design of the High Speed
Train: in the original design the engineers had excelled themselves by cutting down the noise to such a level that it was too
easy to hear your neighbour's conversation and it didn't feel as if
you were really travelling.

Problems with noise disrupting performance often occur
when two or more tasks of different levels of difficulty have to be
done in the same environment. One common example is the
check-in procedure at airports. There the passengers have a very
simple task to do – queue up and check in – and they are
probably nervous while doing it. So a little background music
soothes their nerves and makes them feel better. At the same
time the check-in officers have to do a more complex task –
validating the tickets, reserving seats, helping with changed
booking, etc. – and they often find that the music provided for
the passengers actually disrupts their performance.

Mixing different tasks within the same noise environment is
one reason why so many people dislike open-plan offices. Sometimes the layout of the office is guaranteed to make this happen.
We once saw an attitude survey in which 85 per cent of the
occupants of a relatively new office block said that they found
the noise at their work station intolerable. Dividers – or carrels –
had been erected between the desks, dividing the office into
what the occupants called pig-pens. Investigation showed that
much of their trouble could be attributed to the height of these
carrels which was such that the average person found it comfortable to lean his elbow on the top of the carrel while, say, taking a
telephone call. You might not take all your calls standing up,
though some people preferred to, but this was how you ans-
wered your neighbour's phone if it rang while he was away. The
noise of this call thus interrupted anyone working within earshot. People who work for newspapers or stock exchanges may
find it impossible *not* to work without the noise of fifty other
people doing business within earshot, but most people need
more quiet if they are working with their brains.

Inadequate support on transfer

When I moved down here I found that neither my old manager nor my new one had made arrangements for me to have a desk or chair. Nobody had arranged for me to get an identity badge for the new building, so I couldn't draw expenses or a travel advance. It was four weeks before anyone telephoning me could get through to me. I didn't get the local newsletter. I was supposed to go on a training course the week after I moved; my old manager hadn't informed the new one, so when I got back I got into trouble for being absent and I found that someone had moved my things out of my desk and appropriated it for his own. I was supposed to be invited to a meeting to review my last project but neither my old manager nor my new one saw that I was invited – in fact I didn't even know that the meeting had happened. It's no wonder you start to ask yourself whether anybody wants you.

This is a true account of what happened to someone who was particularly unlucky with a transfer of location in a UK company which is commonly held up as an example of good staff management. Similar problems often arise when people go on secondment to another part of the company, and worse problems occur when they return. It's not uncommon for a person to be given a year's secondment as a career move, for him to do good developing work while away, and for him to return to find that until six weeks previously no-one had given a thought to what should be done with him on his return, and that all he is offered is his old job back. With the benefit of a year's learning it's not surprising that many secondees find their way on to the job market shortly afterwards.

If you have a multi-site operation, or transfer people between departments, you need a check-list of things to do, and who should do them, for the managers involved. Just about all the items you need to cover are implied in the quote at the beginning of this chapter. If you send people on secondment you need someone who has responsibility to monitor the secondment and make arrangements for a suitable job to be available on the return of the secondee. Otherwise you frustrate the expectations which only a little while earlier you took the trouble to raise.

Badly designed tools and equipment

The standard British lathe used to be designed for a double-jointed dwarf with a six-foot armspan. Go into the control room of some power stations and you'll see a magnificent display of dials and digital read-outs that must have looked superb in the artist's impression; you'll also see the wooden packing-case which people drag along the floor so that they can see the top displays, and the masking tape across the windows because nobody thought about the glare. A number of aircraft had to crash into hills before the suggestion – advanced years previously by the psychologist Donald Broadbent – that the clock-style altimeter be replaced by a digital read-out was accepted. Tools and equipment are still sometimes designed with only partial reference to the people who have to use them. A common criticism of British design is that it is component-led; that is, teams of people work on different parts of the final assembly and only come together to integrate their work at a later stage, thus requiring many modifications to produce the final compromise. One reason why European cars and lorries have the edge over some British competition is that they begin the design process by considering how the customer will need to use the vehicle, and work from this initial whole-body concept out towards the individual component design.

People adapt – within reason – to poor equipment. They contrive to get it to work. In the pioneering stages of one's operations there is a good deal of innocent fun to be had in getting poor equipment to work in unsuitable conditions. Problems may arise when they have to change to new equipment, even equipment that on paper looks better. The UK National Institute of Industrial Psychology's survey of *2000 Accidents* showed that many shopfloor accidents were due to small changes in material or tools putting a worker's practised routine slightly out of joint. If your poor performer has been performing badly since moving to a new work station, using new tools, or working on new material, it's worth looking to see if this novelty could be responsible for the performance decline. You may need to be ingenious in your search: did you know that the colour of the curtains in a helicopter can affect its handling characteristics because different dyes affect the fabric's firmness differently, and at the margin this can affect the aerodynamics?

Unsafe working conditions

Regulations about safety and health at work have made it less
likely that people have to work in unsafe conditions. Nonetheless drives to make the workplace safer don't always work, and
the following factors are often to blame:

1. Language and cultural difficulties. It's no good putting up
posters showing white men avoiding accidents if two-thirds of
your workforce are Punjabi women.
2. One kind of accident-prone personality is the rebellious,
anti-authority type. If he sees safety procedures as another
order from management he's likely to rebel against them.
This type responds much better if the work group is given
responsibility for developing its own safety procedures.
3. Safety officers often see their role as that of a score-keeper
('We've gone 254 days without an accident!') rather than an
active preemptor of accidents who needs to be drawn in
whenever new equipment or procedures are considered.
4. Uncertainty about how and when to use shock tactics.
People often quote a piece of research that compared different levels of threat in trying to get people to clean their teeth.
According to the evidence, a moderate threat was more effective than a severe threat. However, against this one must set
the experience of an Israeli factory which has not had an
accident since the safety officer recorded the screams of
someone who had fallen across the circular saw and played
them a few times on the Tannoy. The question of shock tactics
needs better research before one can say conclusively what
works and what doesn't.

Because people adapt to hazardous working conditions it is
often only a change in practice, or the advent of a new worker or
supervisor, which brings the hazards to light. In one factory men
and women worked together and the men would routinely shift
the very heavy weights for the women. A change from hourly
pay to measured day work led to the men ceasing to 'carry' the
women – as they put it – and the women suffered an apparent
drop in performance.

Buildings

Sometimes it seems that more time is lost squabbling over car parking facilities than any other issue, including work. There are other aspects of the building which are worth checking to see if they are inhibiting good performance:

1. Are there enough lifts? Can equipment be moved easily between floors? In a multi-occupancy building are the lifts kept clean and smart?
2. Is the security good and equitable? Can unidentified people walk in? If people are searched on leaving and entering, does this obviously happen to the managing director as well as to the shopfloor workers?
3. Is the lighting good? Can glare be eliminated? Must people work with bright sun in their eyes? Are there any flickering fluorescent tubes? Are dark corners and walkways lit so people feel secure?
4. Are the lavatories adequate and clean? Can you wash your hands, find clean water to drink out of a cup, etc?
5. Are canteen facilities clean, and are they open at the time people need them? Can you get a light meal as well as a plate of boiled stodge? Do you have to be there by 12.15 or all the good food's gone? Is there accommodation for non-smokers?
6. If people need to use telephones as part of their work, are the telephones adequate in number and in the facilities they offer? This is going to get more important as the UK telephone system creaks into the state where it can offer subscribers the facilities Americans have enjoyed for years; it's easy to put together a sophisticated system which does not do what the user wants (e.g. allowing a secretary to see when the boss has finished a call). Are the telephones comfortable to use, and placed where people (left-handers included) can take notes? Are there payphones to discourage abuse of the company phones?

In large buildings it's often not clear who has responsibility for putting things right once they go wrong; and nothing's more disheartening than continually reporting defects only to find that no-one seems to care. People should know whom to report defects to, and whom to contact if they have any suggestions.

It's unlikely that the poor working conditions we have discussed in this chapter would turn a well-motivated performer into a poor performer by themselves. But they can multiply the effect of other causes, reducing the person's motivation to try harder, making him feel that no-one cares, that in a scruffy building where nothing works he's out of step if he tries harder. Improving working conditions is rarely a total cure for poor performance, because the other contributory factors need working on as well, but they are sometimes the first and most obvious place the manager can start. Not all aspects of working conditions are in the control of the individual manager – if the building's wrongly sited, there's not much he can do. The important thing is to try to experience your people's working conditions as they do sometimes – on busy Saturdays if management normally only work weekdays, on shift, in the crowded office, when it's raining. Then look to see if there's anything in the working conditions that's likely to make a browned-off worker into a turned-off worker.

10 Other factors

There are many other factors which can cause or contribute to poor performance, including some which may be unique to the individuals concerned. Those described here are more widespread.

Family problems

Analyses of the severity of various stress factors place the death of the spouse above all others. It can easily wipe out a year of one's life – a year in which fear, grief, anger, bewilderment, and tiredness overwhelm all other emotions and submerge all other motivations and interests. Work is often prescribed as a solace for grief, and it can help; but it needs to be the demanding, punishing, often physical work that sends you to bed exhausted. Grief may be assuaged by digging up the garden, but redesigning the bought ledger system or chairing twice as many meetings is unlikely to be a solace.

Second only to death in the stress it places on the spouse is divorce or separation. The actual divorce itself may be a blessed relief from an unbearable situation, but there is certain to be some effect on performance at work while the causes build up to a head. After the divorce, the man (usually) has to support his ex-spouse, with the consequent drain on his resources, while the wife (usually) has to look after any children of the marriage. This may affect attitudes to work: why should I work harder, says one man, if most of the surplus will go to the taxman or my ex-wife? While another may try to work twice as hard and panic under the stress.

Problems with looking after children are not exclusive to the deserted wife. In most families it is still the wife who is assumed to have responsibility for looking after the children; and this assumption leads to the further assumption that women will be less reliable workers because they will take time off for children's illnesses. This assumption is so common that it is rarely tested in practice; when it has been some surprises have resulted. One of the major UK banks, for instance, found no noticeable difference between male and female absenteeism records once age and length of service had been taken into account. Other studies have found similar patterns, the problem being that women tend to have part-time employment for short periods in some industries. The pattern of absenteeism is often different, with women taking more short breaks and fewer longer ones, while men take less frequent breaks but are absent longer. Women with family commitments are less adaptable if asked to change their schedules at short notice – to work until five this week, to fly up to Aberdeen tomorrow, to stay behind and get this sorted out. At least, that's what people say; however we find more and more that managers grumble just as much about men in this respect, and certainly there is profound nostalgia amongst some managers of the older generation for the days when you could tell someone to pack his bags and move to Upper Grimsdyke, or Somalia, and he'd obey instantly and tell his family to comply.

Separation from the family can contribute to poor performance, and this almost inevitably happens when someone moves to a new location at the company's request. If the organisational myth has it that you must move in order to get promotion, the double bind is made worse. In one study of the problems caused by frequent relocations we found the following problems:

1. The notice people were given was always too short.
2. This meant that in families with children at school, a working wife, or a house to sell, the husband had no choice other than to go on ahead and live in a hotel, leaving the wife behind until the end of the children's school term, or to work out her notice, and to sell the house.
3. Cash allowances paid to cover the expenses of removal were inadequate; they did not cover extra expenses such as new school uniforms, taking into account the fact of not being able to hand down old uniforms.
4. The family met at weekends only with too much to do and different emotional needs. Much of the weekend was spent in house-hunting, but while the husband was tired from the new job the wife and family wanted him to be outgoing and make up for a week's lost family activity, and to help with important family decisions.

5. After a series of moves people felt insecure, as if they dared not commit themselves to liking a house or district too much because they knew they would soon be moved on.
6. The wife's career was usually ruined after a series of moves, unless she was lucky enough to have the kind of job where it didn't matter where she worked. Besides the bitterness this caused in itself, some wives said that the only identity remaining to them was that of their husband's position; they had lost all achievement of their own, and the only stable society and status they had was with other members of the same firm.

These were moves solely within the United Kingdom. Moves abroad can be even more stressful, depending on the couple. It seems to be an unfortunate fact of life that employees are offered career moves abroad just at the time when their families are young and developing. For a young couple with no ties, a couple of years in Australia or Morocco can be exhilarating, the high point of their life; the same couple with two young children could find even six months in the Philippines an intolerable strain. Companies vary greatly in the support they offer; some assume that a good wife will follow her husband wherever he commands, others assume that by asking the whole family to move they have taken on responsibility for the whole family's welfare.

More and more, companies are finding it difficult to get people to move. There are some favoured locations which are worth thousands a year, judging by the promotions people will forgo in order to stay there. Some companies believe that they will have to come to terms with the effect on a husband's career of his wife not wanting to move; we know very few who are actually contemplating what they will do if the husband asks for a move because his wife has been offered a better job elsewhere.

Moving, then, is a time of trial. But why do people move? Because they have been offered promotion or a better job. And it's just at this time of trial that they have to prove themselves worthy of the trust placed in them when they were selected. It's no wonder that many a blue-eyed wonder boy fails in his first few weeks to live up to his promise.

Home circumstances

It's amazing how many cases of apparently unsatisfactory performance were resolved by the introduction of flexible working hours. Instead of forcing people to clock on and clock off at specific times, many employers now offer the choice of arriving and departing within a specified band of time, as long as the correct total number of hours are worked in a given period. Transport to work in the rush hour is prone to disruption whatever mode you use. Would your view of someone as a poor performer be changed if you changed some fixed notions about the correct time to arrive and depart?

In homes where people have been unemployed for a long time it is easy to get out of the habit of regular early rising. There was much fuss made in the tabloid newspapers a while ago because a clerk in an employment office bought someone an alarm clock; the officer pointed out quite reasonably that if this helped establish and reinforce the work habit then the taxpayer was getting quite a bargain. People coming into work from a long time on the unemployment register sometimes have difficulty with other disciplines involved in getting to work; getting clothes out or putting tools to hand the night before, keeping paperwork tidy, not getting drunk the night before if this will affect performance, etc.

Poor eating habits contribute to poor performance as well. The no-breakfast, coffee-and-bun, lunch-with-beer habit is difficult to break, but it's pretty well guaranteed to produce a dangerous drop in blood sugar at mid-morning and mid-afternoon. The blood sugar levels are so low that tiredness and lassitude set in. It's made worse if you have to spend the afternoon in a hot stuffy room without any opportunity for activity. Organisers of conferences or seminars know that the after-lunch session had better contain some activity or people will simply drop off to sleep. Would that more of them provided the option of a light lunch instead of the obligatory stuffing and swilling that seems to be the only atmosphere in which people can approach the serious business of earning a living.

At the other extreme, the eating patterns of shift-workers leave a lot to be desired. Working shifts disrupts the internal clock anyway, so people may not feel like eating at the time they need to. Many shiftworkers leave home unfed – 'I just can't face anything when I get up' – and when they arrive at work they find no facilities for hot food or even a hot drink. They keep themselves going on sandwiches and crisps until the shift is over, when they go home for a hot meal and what sleep they can get. At the time they're working, their stomachs are empty or filled with stodge; then they go to sleep with a full stomach, thus ensuring a bad effect on both sleep and digestion.

Attitudes and ethical problems

'I don't see why I should put myself out until this country has a fully integrated transport system', said a British Railways travel clerk on a training course. The trainer told him not to be so silly. There are other circumstances – easier to sympathise with – where ethical or attitudinal problems may contribute to poor performance. One study in an explosives factory attributed a sudden decline in performance to their *not* having had an accident for a long while – people thought that their luck was bound to run out sooner or later, and as there had been no accident for a while the next one would be a big one.

Some people perform badly because they honestly believe that what they are doing is wrong. Plain refusal is probably less common than bungling – forced to do something which seems to them wrong, most people do it badly. Some questions are simple ethical decisions – should we continue to sell this drug? Fiddle our internal transfer pricing? Not hire blacks? Others are not so simple – should we recommend only the policies/holidays/suppliers who give us the biggest discounts? Allow our agents to offer bribes? Say the boss is with a customer when he's out to lunch?

Few people would choose deliberately to work for an employer they dislike, or in a business they find unethical. Sometimes people find themselves in this position as a result of a takeover or merger. We used to visit a company that had had seven takeovers in eight years, and there were never fewer than seven separate tables occupied in the dining room at lunchtime as the old identities and standards were preserved.

There are ethical problems in the definition of poor performance. Were the people who blocked the payment of compensation to the victims of thalidomide until the children were adolescent and their parents in shreds poor performers or brilliant negotiators? Is the man who, convinced that his organisation is profligate with the ratepayers' money, gives chapter and verse to the media doing a good job or performing poorly? Is the manager who hands back part of his budget unspent at the year end a better manager than the one who over-spends – when both of them know that this year's budget will be positively correlated with what they spent last year? It is not given to many people to partake in the really explosive ethical problems, but most people have to question their values at some time in their lives; whether to keep quiet or be open; whether to let people make mistakes or rush in and correct things for them; whether to spend a few thousand on a safety precaution that's only marginally necessary; whether to put in a low bid with an escalator clause or be honest from the start about what it'll cost. There are genuine dilemmas here, where the employee could be doing well by one set of standards and poorly by another.

Cultural differences

Someone may be judged a poor performer because his attitude to work has been conditioned by different cultural expectations. This area is one where anecdote abounds and serious research is difficult to find. One obvious cultural difference is religion; some religions impose prayers at certain times of the day, impose dietary restrictions which affect performance, regulate who may associate with whom, or dictate what must be worn even if it interferes with safety. We have worked in Northern Ireland for years, loving every minute of it, and find an equal (though sparse) distribution of religious bigots on both sides of the sectarian divide and religious rivalry occurs all the way up the organisational ladder, from shopfloor to management.

Other cultural differences manifest themselves in ways as diverse as competitiveness on the one hand and ability to follow flow-charts on the other. Navajo Indians like to go for a run, but don't see much point in racing – what's the sense in trying to run faster than anyone else? Inhabitants of certain parts of East Africa, for example, where straight lines play a very small part in the visual environment, often have difficulty following visually presented data where straight lines are part of the symbolism. Most Anglo-Saxons agree that French logic is different from theirs, and it's interesting to see how many multinational companies need to use different administrative procedures in France and in the French-speaking parts of Belgium. And the British style of amateurish under-selling diffidence is not well received in the workaholic American eastern seaboard.

On a smaller scale, organisations impose their own culture, which may get people into trouble when they change employers. The house style for the presentation of data, conduct at meetings, who can invite whom to what, how to dress – they all vary, and an insecure employer may see them as wrong, instead of just different.

To summarise this section of the book: poor performance can be caused by a wide variety of factors. It's likely that more than one factor is at work in any one person, and that hardly anyone is an all-round performer. To try to improve poor performance therefore means trying to understand what it is about the individual in his situation that makes poor performance – and its resulting low self-esteem – seem to him to be his best option. Once you understand the problem, you also need to know who *owns* it – not who *caused* it, though this information may be useful in preventing further outbreaks. You need to know whom the problem is hurting; and how to make it hurt the performer so much that he wants a solution – a solution that involves change for the better.

PART III

REMEDIES

11 Counselling and disciplinary interview

Nobody should be identified as a poor performer without his being told. This is a statement of somewhat pious intention; it's what should happen rather than what does happen. The reality of many organisations is that they tolerate poor performers because it would be too much trouble to deal with them before they reach the critical stage and become a real menace. However, if you want to take action to improve someone's performance, the odds are you will want to involve him in the effort; it's difficult to improve really poor performance (particularly when it's one poorly-performing individual in an otherwise satisfactory group) by stealth.

So whatever method of improving poor performance you select from the chapters in this part of the book, you will have to start with a counselling and maybe disciplinary interview. In many cases this is enough to start the improvement – and a self-organised improvement is likely to be more effective than anything you can do outside, though the improvement may need your help and guidance.

In this chapter we discuss some of the skills and strategies a manager needs when conducting a counselling and disciplinary interview. First, though, there are some background considerations which may affect the way he goes about the task.

Is the interview timely?
Here we are asking whether you have decided to take action as soon as you are sure that poor performance has started to occur and will continue if you do nothing; or whether you have let things slip and wish now to reinforce standards which you should have imposed more firmly before; or whether you are taking over from another manager who has let things slip (and who may have been removed from his post for just this reason). When things have been let slip it is more difficult to take action. The lower standards come to be tolerated by the rest of the work group, and may infect the whole of the work group so that instead of one poor performer you have six. If you are replacing

a previous manager, you may have to overcome the feelings of affectionate contempt with which most work groups regard a manager who lets them go slack. Whether this slackness has occurred in your own or the previous manager's time, the best way to start afresh is to begin by some group standard-setting if possible, outside the context of any particular performance problem. See if you can get the shop steward or the employees' unofficial spokesman on your side. If he sees in the eventual outcome a prospect for better bonuses or promotion opportunities for the group he may cooperate. Then in the group meeting try to re-establish a common agreement on the jobs that have to be done and the standards people should work to. Don't appear to be imposing discipline for its own sake; instead make it clear that you wish to re-establish what the job is all about. And if you are taking over from someone else, don't refer back to the previous manager and blame him for everyone's shortcomings or say: 'You thought you could get away with it when he was around, but I'm a different story.' If you want the employees to believe that in their hearts, your actions must speak for you, not your words. What you *can* say if anyone refers to 'new brooms sweeping clean' is that you are not going to let the previous manager's evaluation of their performance stand, and everyone may start again with a clean sheet.

Once you have established a joint agreement on standards, the problem of dealing with any one poor performer becomes a great deal easier, as you can refer back to the standard-setting exercise and make it clear that you believe he knew what was expected of him. If you don't have the standard-setting, but just go in fighting whenever you see poor performance, people will shrug it off as a minor eccentricity, or as a new boy making a lot of noise.

It is much easier to take corrective action if standards have been kept up reasonably well in the past and you move in as soon as things start to slide. Give the person a little time to correct himself – and for you to check that you know what is really happening and have some idea about the cause. Then you can move straight to the counselling interview without the preliminary need to enlist the support of the rest of the work-group.

Have I done everything else first?
You need to check that the poor performance problem is really

what it seems to be, and attributable in whole or part to the person concerned. Have your own standards changed? Have externally-imposed standards changed and the people not been told about this? Is there some change in work environment or content which could be causing the problem? In these cases you may still need to talk to the person – chances are he's unhappy at suddenly becoming a poor performer if it's for reasons beyond his control – but the interview should be obviously labelled as a problem-solving interview, not a counselling and disciplinary one.

You need to check also that you are not taking any action which may prejudice your case in the event of formal disciplinary procedures and maybe dismissal. As we explained earlier, this book is intended to help identify the poor performer and redeem the situation before it reaches the stage of formal disciplinary and dismissal proceedings, so we shall not go into the area of employment law here. But you do need to make sure, by checking with your personnel department, that any actions you have in mind will not prejudice any later action you may want to take if the matter does come to dismissal. They will almost certainly warn you to keep good records, commit things to paper that you might otherwise have chosen just to remember, and make it clear if and when you are giving the person a formal warning. The company may have its own code on dismissals, designed to be stricter than the provisions of the law. If you have moved into a new company with a remit to improve performance, you should check not merely what the law allows you to do, but what the company code expects of you.

Does the job already have standards?
Check whether there has ever been an objective-setting exercise for the person concerned, or whether standards of performance have been laid down for the job. You may then need to question whether these were realistic objectives, and whether the standards had ever been communicated to him. You will then know whether he has any excuse for saying that he didn't know whether he was performing to standard. Sometimes standards get set without anyone knowing about them; we worked for an organisation once where we devoted a lot of time during appraisal training to getting managers to develop standards of performance for different grades of staff, only to find that some-

one in head office had done this exercise – and done it very thoroughly – only eighteen months before, but had forgotten to tell anyone. There are plenty of other cases where you would expect standards of performance to have been set and they have not – we know several retail companies where staff have to stand at counters serving the public, and throughout many reorganisations and fresh designs for the shop layout no-one has ever thought about the speed with which counter staff are expected to process queues, or the number of people who should be in a queue before the supervisor opens up a new position. Or you may find that there are standards of performance, but they are silly beyond words – in one of these companies with counter staff, the number of staff serving was calculated on the average revenue per head, with no account taken of the fact that in one shop they were selling large numbers of low-value goods and in another they sold mainly small amounts of high-value goods.

So, check that standards have been set, and that they seem to you sensible and relevant. See if anyone has ever been through an individual objective- or standard-setting exercise with the person concerned – never mind if it is a couple of years out-of-date. Again, see if you can tell whether the objectives seemed sensible – achievable, capable of success measures, and with an element of personal development.

If you have no evidence that anyone has ever tried to develop standards of performance and objectives for the job concerned, it is worth deciding whether your best approach to the problem performer would in fact be to develop some standards with the group as a whole. This inevitably means postponing the time when you can deal with him as an individual, but at least you will then be able to make reference to group-agreed standards and to claim the implicit support of the work group for your attempt to get him working to these standards. If in your judgement you cannot afford the time this will take, because the performance is deteriorating so badly, then you must spend extra time and skill at the beginning of your interview establishing standards of performance with him.

We don't mean to imply that if you have no written standards, then you have no standards at all. Most people doing a job know what good performance and bad performance feels like, and men of goodwill will usually make an honest assessment of their own performance. Where you have written standards, especially group-evolved ones, your position as manager is made slightly easier: your discussion starts by looking at what *he* considers the necessary standards for the job, but if you cannot agree you know that you can always bring up the previously-established standards and refer to them as a benchmark. If you do not have written standards you must work to establish agreement on the unwritten standards – but the unwritten standards are there, never fear, in every case except that of the person who is completely new to the job and maybe to the organisation as well.

Who else is a party to this problem?
Before you take action you must review the other people involved. You may need their support, or you make take action which will affect them. We set out below the other people who may be involved.

Firstly, there may be other managers, with or without a formal reporting relationship with the person concerned. You are a lucky manager if your own performance is not dependent to some extent on the performance of people who do not report directly to you. Sales targets are affected by the behaviour of service engineers; production targets are affected by the behaviour of the accounts department; the people in recruitment are affected by what the people in basic training do. If you are really unlucky you will find yourself with a day-to-day responsibility for controlling the work of people who have neither direct nor 'dotted line' relationship to you. If the poor performer is so placed that you are not his full-time dedicated manager, you have a difficult negotiation on your hands establishing responsibility for counselling and correcting him. The manager closest to him in daily work is probably the best equipped for the guidance and discipline required, but if he is not acknowledged as the person ultimately responsible for the poor performer, why should the poor performer listen?

Situations like these are usually so tangled that it is difficult to give general guidance; they usually occur in big organisations or firms that are geographically spread out, and they are one of the few good reasons we know for having a reorganisation. The key point is that if you are to try to take action to improve performance then you must be seen as legitimate by all concerned. So you must first approach the other managers concerned and get them to delegate to you the authority for dealing with this particular performance problem. If necessary, they must delegate it to you formally, in front of the people closely affected – the poor performer himself, and his union or other representatives.

You need to establish also, as with any other form of delegated authority, how you will report back on your progress to the manager who gave you his authority to act.

Other poor performers, who may be helping to cause your poor performer's problems, can be divided into those you can influence directly, and those outside your own influence – in another department, perhaps. When there are other poor performers in your own department remember that you must be seen to be fair; you should not act on one without dealing with the others as well.

Where you believe that your poor performer's problems are due in part to the poor performance of someone somewhere else in the organisation, it's worth asking if the two people have ever met, and do they know their work interrelates? Taking the people from the provinces to head office, so that they can meet the voices on the end of telephones and talk to the people who process the paperwork has sometimes put an end to a performance problem – somehow it never really sinks in if you are merely *told* that head office need the figures in by the 12th of the month, or that shifting delivery dates alters schedules all along the line, whereas actually to go and see the work being processed makes a great difference.

You should also be clear about the way your poor performer can and should influence the poor performer in other departments who are exacerbating his problem. Your poor performer may be happy to take the morning off waiting for the work to come through, or he may decide to try to chase it up; you and he will both need to know what he can do to influence the other departments formally and informally. Then, if at the interview he says that he can't do anything because he depends for his work on so many other people down the line doing theirs, you will know (a) whether this is true, (b) whether he can influence it, and (c) what options you have prepared for him to make his task of influencing the other people easier.

If your poor performer is being made worse because of someone else in your own department, you have to decide whether to treat them separately or together. If the whole department is not up to scratch, then you need to look at one of those books on 'How I joined General Universal and turned £3 million loss into £15 million profit'. If you just have one or two, then keep reading. If your two or three poor performers work together, then you probably have no alternative but to treat them as a group at some part of the corrective process. The arguments *against* dealing with people in groups are (a) they can reinforce each other while you're not there, (b) you are setting up mini-negotiating groups and this may go against your firm's industrial relations policy, and (c) you encourage them to make spurious comparisons of one against another, or to say 'I'll move when he moves'. So always start by seeing people as individuals. You might want to arrange the timing of this so that you see them for interview one after another, all on the same day, with no opportunity to confer amongst themselves in between. Be sure to stress the responsibility they each have as individuals for improving their own performance. Later on, when you are looking for things they can do to improve performance, you may want to set some joint tasks and do some joint standard-setting; but always begin by dealing with people one at a time, as individuals.

Other people affected by your problem performers may need to be taken into consideration, or drawn into your confidence. For example, you may give the group leader special responsibility for helping you improve the poor performer – ask him to check more often than he would, to offer help and assistance, etc. You may need to ask the indulgence of people in other departments – 'John's trying a new way of doing his job and I'd be grateful if you could forgive us the odd gaffe while he tries to get it right. I'll try to make sure that the problem doesn't last for long.' Certainly your own manager should know what you are doing, and maybe the personnel department (for information or assistance).

Other people may see themselves as having an interest in what you are doing to correct poor performance, whether you want them to feel this or not. Union representatives may feel it's their territory. Other people in the work group may feel threatened. You would be unwise not to take this into account in your planning.

Unions vary so much in their attitude towards poor performance that it is difficult to give general guidelines, especially as in the UK we have formal union power and policy, and informal power and policy which may react quite differently. There are usually offences which the union formally regards as grounds for instant dismissal – like drinking on duty where this puts lives in danger – but there have been cases where the local people have gone on strike in support of someone who turned up to work paralytic. So you must know not only the formal attitude of the union, but the attitude of your local union representatives as well. You must also work out what arguments will appeal to them if they get interested. Protection of group bonuses, protection of the group's good name, protecting the group against absorption into another group (with a different shop steward and maybe a different union), safety and health at work – these are arguments more likely to appeal to the shop steward than arguments about keeping up 'management' standards or company profits.

In most cases, you want to avoid the issue becoming the subject of an 'official grievance'. An official grievance becomes like an albatross around the neck; it hangs around, gets in the way of solving things informally, and demands formal procedures and representation. Middle management and professional staff rarely use formal grievance procedures, but you need to make sure that you do not push things to the point when they feel they would like to. Make sure that you know your firm's procedure for involving shop stewards or supporters in disciplinary proceedings. You do not want to take any action which could bring the joint wrath of the union, the shop steward, *and* the personnel department on your head.

These preliminary considerations, together with thoughts about the causes of the performance problem, should give you some idea of the strategy to follow in your interview. There are one or two questions outstanding which people sometimes ask:

Do I make an appointment?
The answer here is probably Yes if you are dealing with a long-established problem, and probably No if you are dealing with a sudden deterioration. If you do make an appointment, try to make sure that it is for not too far away – you don't want him to fantasise or to build a case. If on the other hand you decide to speak as soon as you see the standards being breached, make sure that you have had a moment of recollection to think about

the strategy you will adopt, so that you are not seen as just venting your own spleen.

My place or his?

You need to be private, that's for sure; wherever you choose to hold the conversation should be where no-one can listen or see what you are doing (the sight of agitated faces behind glass walls causes all sorts of rumours to start flying). Assuming that you can satisfy these criteria in either place, then the choice of where to hold the interview is governed by the impression you want to create. If you want to make it clear that you are the boss and you have a boss's authority, have it at your place; if you want to convey sympathy and understanding, go to his place.

In any case, the common rules of courtesy apply; suppress the telephone interruptions, make sure there are comfortable seats and writing facilities, offer a cup of tea, etc.

Don't discuss poor performance in public places – trains, planes, restaurants, etc. People sometimes choose these places for this sort of exercise because they think it will be more relaxing to do it over a meal, or to prevent the other person from having the freedom to reveal how he feels. All that happens is that the bitterness lasts longer and is more difficult to cure.

Do I tell him in advance?

The key thing here is to remember that your strategy for the whole of the coming interview is to make it easy for him to do what you want. So don't begin by issuing a challenge which he feels he has to refute. The issue depends on whether you believe that he acknowledges openly to you that he has a performance problem, or whether you believe that you will first have to work at establishing that understanding jointly. In the first case there is no harm in saying: 'I think we ought to talk about this some more when we can give it the time it deserves. How about ten o'clock tomorrow in my office?' In the second case it might be wiser just to say 'Could you step into my office at ten tomorrow, Mike, for an hour or so? Get Carol to cover for you until lunch.'

It's very much better to communicate verbally – face-to-face for preference, over the phone if you must – than to do it in writing. Apart from giving the industrial relations boys a great time if you write letters, there is nothing particularly motivating

in getting a letter saying 'Some time I would like you to explain
to me what went wrong at Croydon'.

Two golden rules

In a counselling and discipline interview there are two golden
rules which you should try to follow at all times. They really will
make the difference between your being in control and your
being driven by the situation.

The first is to *make it easy for him to do what you want*. This
seems obvious, but in fact it's different from what many people
do in practice. They set out to make it obvious that they have
won if the poor performer changes his behaviour; or they set up
a game of 'guess what I want you to do and I'll tell you when
you've got it wrong'; or they throw him in at the deep end to see
whether he's man enough to struggle. All these are fine games if
you like fighting, but if you want your poor performer to change
his present behaviour to something different, it's up to you to
make that change in behaviour as easy as possible.

Making it easy for him to do what you want involves you in
things like: giving him early successes; being prepared to 'trade'
behaviour changes; not making the change in performance a
matter of pride or a challenge to your masculinity; being clear
about standards of performance; not crowing over him when he
has changed – 'I knew you'd feel better once you saw it my way',
is not guaranteed to make the rest of the change simple.

The second rule is to *handle the problem, not the person*. This
rule shows up in a number of ways. It means that you describe
the problem in terms of behaviour, not personality. So you talk
about why Tom has been late eight times out of ten this last
week, and not why Tom is a persistent absentee. You talk about
the fact that labour turnover and grievances are twice as high in
Tom's section as any other, and not about why Tom is so bloody
insensitive. You talk about why Tom's section gets more customer complaints than all the other sections put together, and
not about why Tom's pugnacious attitude upsets the customers.
Sure, it may be that Tom is pugnacious, insensitive, or whatever,
but the point is that from the counselling point of view it is much
better to talk about what Tom does than what Tom is. There are,
in fact, so many good reasons for talking about behaviour and
not about personality that we shall list them below:

1. It is easier to alter your behaviour than to alter your personality. If you are shy, you can learn to behave as if you were not shy – and maybe some of the shyness will disappear. But a full frontal attack on your shy personality is unlikely to help.

2. It is by the same token easier to counsel someone about what to do differently than about what to be differently. You can give a shy person a short list of things to do next time he finds himself at a party which will help him break the ice. It's a lot more difficult to think of advice you can give him about what to *be* differently, unless the advice amounts to: 'It's a good idea not to have that problem and the important thing is to cure it.'

3. It is easier for outside observers to agree about behaviour than about personality. What one person may classify as 'aggressive' someone else may say is 'assertive' and another may describe it as 'anxious'. You would have much less trouble getting these three to agree if what they had to agree on was the number of times the person had interrupted someone else and the number of times he had refused to give way when interrupted himself. This point is particularly important if there will be more than one person involved in trying to improve the poor performance; it is essential that the two or more counsellors talk about the problem in behavioural terms, and not use the more unreliable layman's personality terms.

4. Personality terms will get you into trouble at an industrial tribunal, if things ever get that far. There are a number of judgements making it clear that industrial tribunals are most unhappy when people are dismissed on a case describing not what they did wrong, but how their personality didn't fit.

5. When you talk to someone about what he has done wrong, you can do this in such a way that it still indicates a basic acceptance of and regard for him as a person. 'You're OK, Phil, but you have this problem.' When you talk to him in personality terms, you challenge all of him and reject all of him: 'Phil, you *are* the problem.' Obviously the second method is more likely to antagonise him and make it less easy for him to do what you want.

6. The discipline of handling the problem and not the person is good for you, too. Managers cannot usually afford the

luxury of taking personal dislikes to people who work for them – or, more realistically, they can only afford that luxury at the time of initial selection. If someone's performance is not up to standard you have every right to try to correct it; but if you can't stand his face, you should recognise that the problem is partly inside yourself. If you can't actually say what your poor performer is doing that is detracting from the job in hand, ask yourself whether you need to take corrective action.

7. Finally, if you handle the problem and not the person you both stand a much better chance of being able to measure the success of any changes that come about as a result of your joint efforts. You can measure behaviour, and behaviour change, much more easily than you can measure personality and personality change.

So, we counsel that you should discuss behaviour, and not personality. There is one more dichotomy here – not such a clear one as the problem/person one, but something that managers in certain functions need to be aware of. This is the dichotomy between *behaviour* and *results*. If you are not accustomed to looking at behaviour, you may be concentrating too hard on results and forcing your people into bad performance habits.

What do we mean? Well, the simplest cases are to be found in sales management – the management of the sales function in organisations selling complex equipment or services. Often the only measure they have of their salesmen's performance is the month-end figures. Month-end figures down? Then we have an Early Closing Day, or a Sign-a-Million Day, or some other device for getting the orders in – which is alright if you are selling cheap goods where the customer may give you some money to go away, but detrimental to good customer relations if yours is the kind of business which needs several calls before the salesman and the customer have fully explored the customer's needs.

A manager who is too hungry for the month-end figures, because these are the only results his own boss will understand, could class as a poor performer a salesman who was unwilling to prejudice a good long-term relationship for the sake of pressuring the customer into an early order. The manager stands less chance of making this error if he can ask himself not only about results (for of course we're not saying that results don't matter) but also about the way the salesman behaves when he calls on customers. Is he good at asking questions? Is he good at making the customer's needs explicit? Does he give a lot of product feature statements, or does he wait until he has got explicit needs out and then give benefit statements? If the manager were capable of looking for these behaviours as well as the month-end results, he might be able to turn round to his boss and say: 'Peter isn't due for a reprimand because he didn't get his order signed by the end of last week. I went with him to the customer and judging from the depth of his exploration and the way he was really making that customer want a solution, I honestly believe that he'll sign him up before long and it looks like the beginning of a long relationship between Peter and that customer.'

Discuss results by all means. Consistently poor results show that there is something wrong. But you should know what the person did to achieve those poor results or you should know what questions to ask him to find out; and you should not be bemused by over-concentration on short-term results if yours is not the kind of operation that works purely in the short term.

Strategy for the counselling interview

A counselling interview should follow this plan:

Agree standards
Agree that there has been a gap
Agree the size of the gap
Agree who has responsibility for reducing the gap
Agree on actions to reduce the gap
Agree measures and time for reducing the gap
Set time for follow-up meeting.

In following this pattern the skilled manager will use a lot of these behaviours:

Asking questions
Testing understanding
Summarising.

Easier said than done. If all you had to do was let him know you were not pleased with his performance, we could have written:

Tell him the standards
Tell him there has been a gap
Tell him the size of the gap, etc.

But you have to get him to agree with you that there has been a
gap and that he could do something about it. Tactically, the best
way to get him to agree with you is for you to agree with him.
So . . . ask questions.

Take these various stages one at a time:

Agree standards

In your preparation for the counselling interview you should
have found out whether any standards have ever been set for the
job, or any objectives set for this particular job-holder. If there
are, have them in reserve. You want to begin with questions
like: 'Tell me in your own words, Alan, do you think you have
been performing up to standard lately? What do you think the
standards should be in your job?' You can bolster this if you like
with other questions, like 'Give me an idea of how somebody
who was really good at this job would do it . . . how someone
who was averagely good would do it . . . how someone would do
it who had not had the proper training or experience.' You want
to get him talking about the kinds of standards he expects to
apply to the job, almost without reference to his own particular
performance. While he is talking, be alert for the standards he
gives high priority to; you want answers to questions like:

1. Does he believe that quality or quantity of work is the
most important factor?
2. How does he see the relative priorities of the different
parts of his job (e.g. dealing with the customers/doing his
accountancy/planning ahead)?
3. How does he view the relative priorities of the different
people who can call on his services?
4. Does he differentiate at all between work that is important
and work that is merely urgent?

Questions you can use to help establish these facts include: 'Is
the job getting easier or more difficult? How?' and 'Do you have
trouble deciding what to do first?' and 'Do you have difficulty
handing over your job to someone else when you go on holiday,
say, because they do it so very differently from your way?'
Explain that you are trying to build up a picture of his under-

standing of the standards of performance for the job. Make notes – there's nothing wrong in making notes, as long as you make them fairly continuously; stopping to note down points that incriminate will soon clog the flow of the conversation, but a continuous and open note-taking to which he feels he can contribute himself will help. So, draw up your picture of the standards in whatever form seems best. Then you can bring out the existing standards or objectives, if you have them – not in any spirit of triumph, but to check as a matter of interest how your joint standards agree with or differ from the ones already set. Ask him which picture – or an amalgamation of the two – he is prepared to accept for his own job. If he suggests that the standards be bent because of present difficulties – difficulties which you suspect he wishes to use as excuses for not doing the job properly – make it clear that you are trying to establish a set of standards in the absolute sense, so that you can make modifications where necessary, but you would rather not build up a set of standards around unusual circumstances.

Before you move on to the next stage, summarise. Write your summary if necessary. In one or two sentences, or a diagram or two, compress the sense of the discussion and agree the main performance standards for the job.

Agree that there has been a gap
The simplest way to do this is by the question: 'Tell me, John, do you believe that you have been performing up to these standards lately?' He'll probably begin by lacing his agreement with a powerful dose of excuses; make it clear that while you may want to return to these later, all you are concerned to do at the moment is to establish that he agrees that he is failing to meet the current job standards. Usually you will get a grudging agreement, accompanied by the statement that everyone else does it, or he doesn't see it as so serious, or things have been better, or he's been doing so much better in another area of his job that he thought it was OK to neglect this one. Make it clear that you are dealing here with him alone; comparisons with other people are not part of the agenda and if other people have been falling down then you know about it and will want to deal with it too.

If you do not get even the grudging agreement, then you must start to itemise the failures you have seen – expressing them in behavioural terms, of course. Each one may have its own excuse; remind him that you are not interested now in excuses, though later you may be concerned to remove any obstacles to good performance which he wants to tell you about; right now all you are concerned to do is to establish what did and did not happen.

The examples you cite, at least at first, should be recent ones. You do not want to give the impression that you have been keeping a 'little black book' of failures for just such an occasion as this. You can refer later to the fact that the problems seem to have been growing for some time, if this is appropriate.

Be alert to any genuinely contradictory evidence, as opposed to excuses, which he may offer. There may have been areas he has been working on which you do not know all about, or instructions he received from other sources which change your opinion about the existence or the size of the gap.

Agree the size of the gap
By now, he's probably feeling pretty miserable. It's obvious to him that you have decided to tackle his performance problems from the ground upwards. You're not going to accept any of his excuses, tales of mitigating circumstances, hiding behind other people's skirts. You've made it clear that you have been looking dispassionately at his performance lately, and found it wanting. You have two more things to do in the task of defining this gap. You have to agree about its size, and you have to make it hurt. Yes, hurt – because at the moment as far as he's concerned, you're the one who hurts most. You're the one who's uncovered all the evidence of wrong-doing. You're the manager – it's your problem. He may be miserable because of what he knows you know, but the problem still hurts you more than it hurts him.

In agreeing the size of the problem, you must also make the ownership of the hurt change places. You must:

(a) agree the *areas* of the performance which have been unsatisfactory, and the areas of performance which remain satisfactory;
(b) consider the implications for him, his work, his colleagues, and the rest of the organisation if the unsatisfactory areas are not corrected.

Agreeing the areas where performance is unsatisfactory is easier if you have taken notes. You can then physically indicate where the problems are. In doing this, you should try to give the impression that the problem is a containable problem – he is not damned totally and entirely, there is just this one problem area. If necessary – if he looks intolerably gloomy, or is making the kind of hysterical statement 'You're as good as telling me I have no future in this firm, I may as well pack my bags today', then refer back to the areas where he is performing well (even if you have to work hard to find any) and indicate that the problem is manageable.

Your second task is to make this newly-defined problem one that hurts. You have to make him see the implications of the problem. Up until now – this counts particularly if you are trying to clear up a situation that other people have tolerated – he has been content to live with his problem. We all have problems that we are content to live with. We vaguely know that we should perhaps do something about the ring round the bath, or giving up smoking, or making a will, but the problems don't hurt enough for us to want a solution. You have to make him hurt enough to want a solution. You do this by asking him questions – questions about the effect his poor performance is having on the things he cares about.

For example, you might ask him about the effect his performance has on his colleagues: 'Who usually picks up this extra work, then, Sue? How does she cope? How do you think she feels about it?' Or 'What does this do to the group productivity target, George? Are you sure your problem isn't costing your mates money?' Or 'How many out-of-territory points are you giving Jack a year, then? Wouldn't it be cheaper and quicker to give him the money?' Or you might ask about the effect his performance has on the way other people think about him: 'What sort of difference will this make to your reputation if it goes unchecked?'

Or you could ask about the effect on his pocket: 'When you come to make a return call on this customer and you find you didn't fill in the record, are you going to be able to rely on that customer's goodwill in helping you re-establish what he wants? And if not, how much is this going to cost you?' Or 'Have you calculated the effect on your bonus of having so many returns? How much longer would you have to work next month to make the money back up?' Or you could ask about the effect on his prospects: 'Have you thought what effect this will have on your promotion prospects if it goes unchecked?' Or 'Could this affect your rate of promotion in the future?'

Then again, you could strike at his pride: 'How do you think you compare now with the other graduates who joined at the same time as you did?' or 'Is this problem helping or hindering your long-term ambitions?' Or his loyalty to the organisation: 'Does this affect the impression you give our customers? Could this affect our business?'

Enough of examples. The key is to take the problem and expose all tentacles it extends into the other areas of performance and the other things he cares about – to get him thinking about the *implications* of this problem – and to do it by asking him questions. You can make statements about the implications of the problems: 'I've calculated that this is bringing down the group bonus by 75 pence a week'; but then it remains your problem. Uncover the implications by asking him questions, and you have started to transfer the ownership of the problem and to foster an urgent desire for a solution. If at this stage of the proceedings you can get *him* to summarise what you think you've agreed so far, you are well on the road to action. But don't push him to summarise if he is indicating by his behaviour or emotional state that the problems are too fresh and tender in their implications for him to claim happily as his own.

Agree who has responsibility for reducing the gap
By this stage you have agreed that there is a problem; it is his problem; and it could have far-reaching implications if it were not solved. Your next question must then begin with a phrase like: 'Would it help if . . .?' 'Would it help if we could find a way of bringing your scrap rate under control?' 'Would it help if we could find a way of coping with the administrative load as well as the other tasks? 'Would it help if you knew what your limits of authority were?' 'Would it help if . . .?' Make him want a solution to his problem. Then you have to agree who has responsibility for reducing the gap.

Your aim here, of course, is to get him to claim total or partial responsibility for reducing the gap. The other party who can help is yourself as the counselling manager. Attempts to put the onus onto other people should be firmly resisted.

Questions like: 'Together, Tony, what can you and I do about this?' or 'How do you think you could start to put things to rights?' or 'How can I help you achieve these goals?' help to put the responsibility for change onto Tony's shoulders. The temptation for Tony here is to say that things should never have happened – 'It's no good telling me to supervise them better, they should never have happened – 'It's no good telling me to supervise them better, they should never have been recruited like that', or to say that he can't shift until someone else does – 'As long as I have these lousy products to sell, it's no wonder I can't make quota.' You have to remind him gently but firmly that neither of you can change the past, you have to deal with the present situation for better or worse, and while you are open to his suggestions for preventing problems in other departments the meeting today is between the two of you.

You have a difficult task to do here, because you need to convey to Tony the impression that you are prepared to help him – indeed, you should already have thought about the possible causes and cures for his problem – but you want him to start helping himself first. If you rush in too early, perhaps in response to an appeal – 'You've been a manager here longer than I have, you tell me what I need to do' – then you risk reclaiming ownership of the problem which you have so carefully persuaded Tony to accept for his own. And most counselling managers are tempted to rush in here, because their greater experience and the thought they have given to the problem means that they probably do know better than Tony what course of action to suggest. It's difficult to see someone struggling with a problem to which you know the answer, but you have to steel yourself to do it.

Oddly enough, one of the most useful questions if he gets stuck at this stage is: 'If someone else came to you with this problem, what would you advise them to do? This works time and again, despite its obvious trickery – of course, it helps him distance himself from the problem and look at it in perspective. As soon as you have got him to make some tentative suggestions about what *he* could do, and got him to spell out how they would actually help to solve the problem, you have achieved your aim of getting him to 'own' the problem. It is now OK for you to add solutions of your own, though it's still better if he suggests them and your role is to support, modify, or mould them.

Agree on actions to reduce the gap
The different kinds of actions you both have open to you are reviewed in the remaining chapters of this book. They boil down to: changing the job in whole or part, training him, offering counselling at a deeper level than you as an amateur can manage, enlisting the support and pressure of his peers, and changing the organisation. These are formal actions that usually involve spending time and resources on a generous scale. Before you embark on any of these actions, consider whether the interview you have now had seems to have helped. Maybe the clarification of standards and priorities was all that was needed. Maybe there are informal things that you or he could do as part of the daily job that would help. Can you help him with his record-keeping, or his planning, or his priority-setting? Can you help by clarifying his role in meetings or giving him specific tasks to do? Only a limited number of cases of poor performance require action as drastic as changing the job or spending money on training.

The more you can keep the responsibility for improving performance and the necessary actions as a private bargain between you, the better the chances of things actually improving. Only involve outsiders or formal changes if you are certain that they will add to what you as a manager are already doing. It will help the poor performer if you agree to 'trade' with him – for every change he agrees to make, you agree to make one also. And although the responsibility for action must remain with him and you, if you undertake to help smooth out relationships with other people or other departments this will help convince him you're serious.

It's more important than ever to summarise as you reach the end of this stage in the proceedings. You need to state clearly what each of you has agreed to do, and to write it down if necessary – be sure to give him a copy. If you want to, you can make a point of saying that these are the only two copies that will be taken and you will throw yours away if things do get better.

Agree measures and time for reducing the gap
You need to be specific about the time-scale involved, and when you could both expect to see some changes. Try to arrange things so that the projected course of action will generate some changes fairly early on – he needs the quick reinforcement and

feedback from his actions. You also need to agree on the kind of things you will be looking for which will tell you whether things are getting better, in terms of behaviour, or in terms of results, but not in terms of personality. The early work you did in establishing standards will be helpful here, which is why it was a good idea to make notes at the time. When constructing these measures, protect the poor performer's pride. It's not much fun knowing that the rest of the workforce know you're under notice to improve. We have seen managers ruin things at this stage by saying: 'I'll be coming round asking the rest of the group if they are finding you more co-operative.' The measures should be ones that you and he together should be able to observe without shouting from the hilltops that this is what you are doing.

Set time for follow-up meeting
You should have at least one follow-up meeting. Even if things improve and you both informally recognise this, you need the ritual sense of closure that the follow-up meeting provides – the sense that now you have drawn a line underneath the episode and will not need to refer to it again. And you need to say Well done and Thank you. If the improvement takes some time, you will need two or three follow-up meetings which will be mini-cycles of the full counselling and disciplinary interview given here. Don't leave the setting of the next meeting until some notional time in the future while you wait to see how things turn out; fix it at the end of the counselling meeting, so that you both know what sort of improvements have to be made and by when.

In this strategy for the counselling interview we have assumed that things go fairly smoothly – that beyond the normal set of excuses you are both on the same side with the same interests. Suppose things don't go as well? Suppose he won't talk, or he gets abusive – how do you react then? There are some behaviours you can use which will help in these difficult situations.

When he won't talk, ask 'open' questions – that is, questions which demand a fuller answer than Yes or No. Open questions usually beginning with words like 'how' or 'why' or 'tell me more' are more likely to get a response than 'Is the problem X or Y?'. It's usually possible to block one open question, but not two:

'How do you feel about the way the work's been going lately?'
'I don't know, really.'
'How's it progressing, though?'
'Oh, well, I suppose it could be better.'
'In what way could it be better?'

and you're away. The temptation for most counsellors is to get dismayed after the first reply and leap in with a closed question or one that suggests the answer and will not get him talking: 'I suppose the new work rota's the problem?' Asking open questions and then getting him to clarify preferences and value judgements is the way to start dealing with the low reactor.

When he talks too much, ask questions which he can only answer with a Yes or No or a specific piece of information, e.g.

'So if I can interrupt a minute, are you saying that it was the new delivery that caused the problems?'
'Yes, like I said, it was full of –'
'And when exactly did the new delivery arrive?'
'Friday morning, just when we were –'
'What time Friday morning?'
'It must have been about eleven o'clock, because –'
'And who took delivery of it?'
'Rattigan, took it without checking or anything, like I said, he's in league with –'
'Was there a delivery note?'

Questions like these, demanding short specific answers, help to close down the person who is being over-talkative. Take care in using them, of course; sometimes their over-talkativeness is a way of settling down and coping with nervousness, or it will provide clues to what really is going on; but if it's just being used as a smoke screen to prevent you both from seeing the real issues, then use closed questions to re-establish control of the conversation and come to the point.

Handle generalised abuse either by ignoring it completely, or by the 'fogging' technique – mild agreement, or plain repetition, with *nothing else added.* Two examples of 'fogging'

'It's mostly your fault – you're such a lousy delegator.'
'I'm a lousy delegator.'

and:

'None of this would have happened if you'd sent me on that course I asked for.'

'You could be right, none of this would have happened if I had sent you on that course you asked for.'

The key skill is to send his message back to him, totally reflected and unaltered – which is why it's called 'fogging', it's what happens when you shine a light on fog. If while you do it you sit square on to him, looking relaxed, using a neutral tone of voice, pausing slightly before you say anything, the effect on him will be quite remarkable. You've just parried his attack, while he was expecting you to try to counter-punch. He's got no way of responding to what you've said, because you haven't said anything – you've just reflected his own message back to him. It's a cruel trick to play, because most people flounder most painfully when you use fogging on them, but it's one of the best ways of handling abuse without raising the temperature or losing control of yourself.

Threat works when it is seen as legitimate and backed up by the power to act. It does not work when it is perceived as a challenge, another way of raising the stakes, or as personal spite. If in the last resort you are going to use threat – 'If things don't improve we shall be looking to find ways of parting with your services' – then you must be seen as (a) able to make that threat and carry it out if necessary on your own authority, and (b) making it at the appropriate stage in the discussion when the alternatives are genuinely those of improvement or dismissal, not at the early stages of the interview when you are still both examining the issues and setting your stalls out.

Counselling and disciplinary interviews are delicate things. If they are done well, you have the immense satisfaction of the resulting performance improvement. But they are easy to do badly, and most managers don't get anything like enough training in how to do them. Off-line role-plays help, if you can persuade your training people to run a couple of courses where you actually practise some of the steps involved; make sure that you get practice at both sides of the game – manager and poor performer – and try to use real situations that have happened in your own company. Your own manager, or a good staff adviser, may be able to work through with you the steps involved in a coming disciplinary interview, rehearsing your way through the difficult bits. Try not to do your first one without any preparation at all. And remember the key skills – listening, asking questions, summarising. If it helps, try writing out some of the questions you could use – not to trot them out like a script, but so that the ground is reasonably familiar to you.

To summarise this chapter: the strategy for the disciplinary and counselling interview is to agree that there is a gap between present performance and agreed standards; to make the interviewee want to correct that gap as much as or more than you want it corrected; to agree what he can do, without your help if necessary, to put things right; and to agree follow-up meetings and the measures you will be using. Your style should be firm but supportive, which you will convey by measures such as handling the problem and not the person. And you should try to take opportunities to rehearse in advance the options you have and the kinds of question you might ask.

12 A different job

You may be able to solve your problem performer's difficulties by putting him into a different job. The physical location and content of the job, the social context, or the motivational aspects, may influence you in making this decision. The new job may be up, down, or sideways relative to the old job, and you may find that personnel policies or union agreements restrict your freedom to make the kind of transfer you believe to be appropriate.

What kind of problem might you solve with a change of job? The most obvious problems are those to do with travel and location of work. Sometimes company policy almost forces people to become poor performers without their wanting to, because the policy-makers have not thought out the implications of their decisions. For example, in some firms with a number of London offices no formal account is taken of the difference in travelling time to the different offices, and employees are transferred from, say, Richmond to Croydon without any allowance for the increased travel time and costs. In another organisation – a major UK airline – the company rules say that you must live within 30 miles of Heathrow Airport. In practice this rule is relaxed in the case of people who fly out of Newcastle or Birmingham or Manchester; but the training department haven't heard of the relaxation and refuse to pay people subsistence costs when they are called to training courses located at Heathrow. Silly bits of bureaucracy like this, which eat into people's pockets or their time and build up tremendous resentment, are probably to be found in many firms of any size. It may be easier to alter your starting and finishing times slightly to fit in with local public transport than to waste lots of effort persuading people to stay until the right time.

If you have only one site, then you have much less scope for solving people's problems by changing their jobs. If you run a multi-site operation, do check that you know about vacancies on other sites in the group. Unions are remarkably unforgiving if you fire someone from one job and recruit for a similar job on a different site.

117

Problems with physical working conditions are often helped by a job change, also; sometimes to the same job in a different part of the office or factory. People vary enormously in the extent to which they can tolerate outside noise, flickering lighting, strong sunlight, strange smells, draughts; you may be able to improve performance by taking away some of the distractors. Remember that the experiments which led to the identification of the famous 'Hawthorne effect' took the form of changing the working conditions of a group of assembly line workers, with the result that whatever changes were made, some improvement in performance resulted. Moving someone to a different work station can have the same effect; the extra attention leads to an improvement which you can then try to consolidate.

Moving someone to a new job gives him a new group of people to relate to – a new set of colleagues, new subordinates maybe, a new manager perhaps. There are some cases of plain personal incompatability where this is your only option, if you can exercise it. We know one case where the relationship between a regional manager and one of his district managers is so sour that one has difficulty staying in the same room with the other – yet both are delightful people to meet individually, both are utterly dedicated to the success of the firm they work for, both well thought of by their own colleagues. It would be better all round if one of them could move, but it's unlikely to happen. Unfortunately many companies have a clause prohibiting a manager from passing on to another manager someone who is performing badly. The laudable intention is that people should be responsible for correcting their own failures of management and not push them off onto someone else, but it makes it difficult to achieve transfers where they would in fact be helpful. If someone moves to a new job to try to improve his performance it's important that stories of his previous failures are not bandied about too much. The sending and the receiving manager both need to have their ears to the ground to catch the gossip, and be ready to intercept it if they can. Introduce the new man with some reference to past successes, or his positive skills, or the contribution you expect he will be able to make to the group. Give him a job to do which will bring him into contact with his new working colleagues – preferably one which fosters mutual interdependence. Be sure to have an early performance review with him where you ask how he is finding his new associates.

Moving to a different job also helps when for ethical or political reasons someone does not like the job he has been assigned to. Ideally, you ought to find this out at interview time, but interviews are notoriously unreliable and it sometimes happens that on a second or third transfer the person finds himself doing a job which conflicts strongly with his own value systems. A strong union man could be asked to prepare a case against his own union; a convinced white supremacist asked to work alongside people of a different race; a believer in openness and honesty at all times asked to conduct sensitive negotiations or tell lies to the media. You may decide that in the long run you do not want people of such sensibilities working for your organisation; but in the short term it could pay you to move them to another job.

Sheer mismatch of abilities is probably the single most important reason for removing someone from a job. The move, as we said before, can be sideways, upwards, or downwards. Demotion should be used when someone has clearly been put into a job that is too intellectually demanding or requires skills that he does not have. A high frequency of mistakes, work going unchecked, difficult work being ignored – these things may tell you that the person simply can't cope. If counselling doesn't work, and training is unlikely to bridge the gap, you really have no choice but to reinstate him in his old job or share the workload of the existing job in such a way that the demands on him are less.

In our experience in the UK and Europe, demotion rarely happens in white-collar jobs. In blue-collar jobs and some clerical jobs people are often put into new jobs for a trial period, to see how they shape up, with the option of not continuing if they prove unsatisfactory. In white-collar jobs the trial period isn't used, or it is more difficult to arrange. Even the option of having the new boy work alongside the previous occupant for a few weeks during job changeover is rarely used, though it provides a golden opportunity for training and introductions as well as a trial period for the newcomer. No, the reality still is that people are pitchforked into new jobs, usually after inadequate assessment of their potential and abilities. When they fail it is usually regarded as their fault, and they get demoted or – more often – pushed sideways. It's amazing how in the 1960s and 1970s many organisations grew little 'zombie slots' – nothing jobs which people were put into because they had made a hash of a real job but the company didn't want the trouble of demoting them. As pressures intensify for leaner and more efficient organisations, these zombie slots are gradually disappearing but not before a great deal of harm has been done.

There are, of course, good things you can do to minimise job failure due to lack of basic abilities. A well-designed performance appraisal system helps. So does using trained interviewers and a structured interview when people apply for jobs. Psychological testing of skills and abilities, as well as of personality and motivation, is becoming more widely accepted. Assessment and development programmes actually build mini job situations where it becomes apparent whether people have the potential to do the job well, and whether money invested in training and development would be well spent. But if you are faced with the consequences of *not* doing these things, it's probably better to demote the person, admit publicly that it was as much your fault as his for not assessing him correctly, and making it your top priority to find him a more suitable job move in the future.

Genuine moves sideways – as distinct from moves into zombie slots – help when someone's mix of abilities is not right for the job, although his level of ability and motivation may be acceptable. Most people would recognise that there are typical good line men and good staff men, and that you wouldn't put a staff man in a line man's job, nor vice versa. That is by no means a universal rule, but it does indicate a trap for the unwary. A line manager who likes pressure, likes taking quick decisions, likes having a number of things going on at once, and is more concerned with the short term, could well go to pieces if you put him in the strategic planning department where he has to sit with an empty desk, some books and papers, the telephone numbers of a few experts, and the expectation that it'll take him six months to produce a report. The professional turned manager often has this difficulty too: many professionals get very discontented if they are asked to turn away from their own work to manage and control the work of other people. More and more companies are adopting professional career paths, giving equal esteem and status for equal professional rather than managerial contribution, so that they create fewer performance problems in this area. The professional/manager dichotomy creates real problems in organisations such as the Civil Service, where it is not in fact recognised as a dichotomy; if you are a scientist in the Civil Service you find that as you advance further up the ladder more and more managerial tasks are heaped upon you, until your professional contribution fades away under the pressure of organising and controlling other people's work. When we have worked inside the Civil Service we have found more identified performance problems (identified by the management, that is) at Principal Scientific Officer level than at any other; it is not surprising to learn that this is the level at which people experience the most serious tussle between the professional and the managerial sides of their job – and since they mostly didn't covenant for the managerial side when they joined, it's no wonder they grumble.

Promotion for poor performers? Why on earth should we want to advocate that? Because there are plenty of cases where people are hired to do a job that is in fact too small for them, and they fret and do badly under the frustration. With the slowdown or standstill in growth that many companies are experiencing at present, underplacement is a more common problem than it used to be; and sometimes managers compound it by saying 'They should be glad of a job – any job'. If you suspect that someone is performing badly because his abilities are being under-used, remember that in the first part of this book we discussed the difference between knowing how to do your work, and knowing how to plan it so that it fits in with what everyone else does. You need to decide whether the reason for the poor performance lies in the lack of challenge in the actual work content, or in the person not being able to plan his work to best advantage; the two things need different kinds of treatment, and you could make the problem worse by treating the wrong cause.

An example of underplacement due to lack of challenge in the job content is a secretary who was on the point of being fired when she was assigned to a new boss. The staff manager offered the boss his sympathies – the secretary couldn't concentrate, skimped her work, gossiped with the other girls, and was generally a bad influence – and since she was one of the longest-serving secretaries her influence was quite strong. The new boss had a long talk to her, and decided that the reason for her poor performance was the fact that she could do her work comfortably in half the time allotted. So the new boss effectively redesigned her job to make her into a personal assistant, and within a very short time applied for an upgrading for her on the grounds that her work had improved out of all recognition.

Underplacement caused by knowing what to do, but being unable to plan how it fits in with the rest of the organisation, is seen in many graduate appointments and recruits from other organisations. It's a particular problem with people recruited into staff departments, where the relationship with the line has to be negotiated differently in different functions and different firms. A good example here is the internal consultant who was very highly thought of outside his firm, but regarded as useless by the people inside – who only kept him on because his books and reputation were good for them in a general kind of way. He had little trouble negotiating outside assignments, but had no idea how he ought to get people inside using his services –should he push himself forward or wait to be asked? Should he try to work through divisional directors or be available to anyone who asked for his services? How could he put priorities on the tasks he was asked to achieve? How should he charge for his services? How should he liaise with other staff departments? You can argue, of course, that a good internal consultant would get these things ironed out; but the reason he was a poor internal consultant lay in his inability to put his own job into the context of other people's, not because of any lack of skill when it came to face-to-face consultancy assignments. It's likely that the move to a different job better suited to one's skills and abilities will help with the first kind of underplacement; the second kind is more likely to need the help and counselling of the manager while keeping the person in the existing job. So you must be sure whether the problem is due to a real work underload – in which case move to a more demanding job – or due to work underload because the person can't manage the interface between his job and those of the people round him.

Moving someone to a new job as a way of coping with poor performance works best with younger people. The older you are, the less chance there is of getting into the simple misplacement problem (because people get better at choosing jobs as they get older) and the less easy it is to accept that you must put the past behind you and try again. Some firms have policies which help prevent this kind of performance problem; other firms have policies which might have been designed to cause these problems.

An example of the latter is the graduate recruitment programme run by one large UK manufacturing company. Graduates here are put into a career stream on joining – you are
expected to choose between manufacturing, personnel, accountancy, etc. – and once in your career stream it is very difficult to
change. Despite the fact that most surveys agree that good
managers need a variety of functional experiences early in their
career, and despite the common view that it's difficult to predict
in advance what kind of career you will find most suitable, this
firm insists that once you have chosen, you stay with it. Not
surprisingly, their rate of loss of graduate trainees is huge, and
they blame the graduates for their lack of 'stickability'.

By contrast many more enlightened companies run schemes
where new recruits are exposed to a variety of different jobs in
different functions early in their careers, with every opportunity
to change from the one originally chosen. In one firm there is a
formal graduate training scheme, at the end of which a self-
assessment programme is run to give the graduates and their
potential managers the chance to assess their suitability for jobs
in different functions. The programme consists of a series of
modules; each module is an exercise which brings up some of the
problems and opportunities of working in a particular function,
and it is introduced by a senior functional manager, who stays to
observe the exercise. At the end of the exercise each trainee fills
in a form on which he records his feelings about the exercise and
whether he feels his own skills and abilities are suited for the
function. At the end of the series of modules each trainee has a
dossier which he can use as a basis for counselling with the
training manager, and the functional managers have had a
chance to look at the likely material they will be offered in the
work context as opposed to the interview context. With this
method of selection and placement, the number of early placement errors is considerably reduced and the need to demote,
promote, or move sideways contained at an acceptable level.

Moving someone to a new job to try to correct his poor
performance ought to be an honest exercise. Don't give him the
kind of impossible remit that nobody would be likely to do well.
It may be a tempting cop-out – 'We'll give you one last chance,
there's a golden opportunity selling old Ronald Reagan movies
in Moscow . . .' – but his failure will have a demoralising effect
on all the people he has to deal with, and though you may be able

to use this failure to fire him or persuade him to go, the chances are you'll have a morale problem among the people left behind.

When people move to new jobs, there are always bits of administration left behind which catch up with them later. One of these is the performance appraisal system. Not all firms with appraisal systems have good policies about what to do when people move jobs. It's slightly easier when you appraise on the 'birthday' system – people are appraised on the anniversary of their joining the company, or some other significant date – than if you have an appraisal season where everybody stops doing work and does appraisals instead. If you have the first system, it's easy to install a simple rule that says that no-one shall have an appraisal interview until he has been working for six months at least for his manager. Without such a rule, problems arise about who does the appraisal – the old one or the new one? This is a particularly sensitive problem for the poor performer, moved from one job to another in the hope of improving his performance. There are two issues: the simpler one of who is to do the interview, and the more complex one of how to take into account any improvement that may result from the job change. The question of who does the interview needs a policy decision. The 'no formal appraisal before six months' relationship' is probably the best policy decision, though *informal* appraisals at more frequent intervals are especially necessary when you are dealing with a poor performer. Another way of coping is to say that *both* the managers get involved – the previous one takes responsibility for the backward-looking part of the appraisal and the present one takes responsibility for objective-setting, future planning, training and development needs, etc. The worst way to do it is a method we came across recently – the old manager wrote the appraisal and the new one read it out, solemnly – no opportunity for disagreement or clarification, no reason for either party to feel committed, just the delivery of a charge sheet from your old commanding officer.

How do you take into account the improvement that has (one hopes) started since the change of job? After all, an appraisal is supposed to look back over a year (usually) and if we have poor performance for the first six months, just acceptable performance after the change, and now performance starting to improve, how shall we assign it a ranking or rating? The short answer is, you don't. Use words instead. Managers really ought to feel that they have the freedom to adapt performance appraisal forms to suit unusual circumstances. Some forms don't need much adapting; the IBM appraisal form, for example, had a space where the manager was to record his comments if performance had changed notably over the last six weeks or so. This gave the manager a chance to say if there had been a sudden improvement, so that he could in honesty assign a 'D' rating for performance over the whole year, but indicate that lately performance was up to 'C' standard. That left all parties feeling better and was a more honest record of what had actually happened. You have to balance the motivational effect of the appraisal interview against its purpose as a record of what the performance was actually like. Most appraisal forms satisfy the second purpose without making allowances for the first. It's therefore up to the individual manager to use the record form, adapting it if necessary, so that the poor performer feels that his fresh efforts have been noted: 'I've had to give you a 4– for the whole year, Tom, because I'm supposed to record your performance for the whole year, and we agreed that it wasn't good. But we both know that since you've moved into the new job you have been doing much better, so I've drawn a line on the form here and written in "Performance in last 2 months since transfer, 3+ and continuing to improve". With a bit of luck by the next appraisal we'll be writing down a 2, so shall we talk about how we're going to achieve it?'

13   Job redesign

Job enrichment, or job redesign, can help the poor performer under certain circumstances. The principle is that you keep him in the same post, but change the job content or circumstances to remove some of the factors that contribute to his poor performance. Job redesign can take any or all of the three different aspects described below.

Changed physical circumstances

You may alter the physical location of a job or the environment in which it takes place, and this is particularly useful when dealing with older, disabled, or handicapped workers. Older people find assembly line tasks doubly demanding; as they get older they are both slower to spot their mistakes and slower to correct them, resulting in often massive decline in performance with age. So to reduce scrap, you could slow down the assembly line if there were a great number of older workers on it; or put all the older workers together on a single, slower line (taking action as appropriate to ensure that their morale did not suffer at the thought of being put 'on the shelf'; or take the older people off assembly line duties altogether.

Changing the physical circumstances of a job may mean nothing more elaborate than altering the office furniture. Bad lighting, uncomfortable chairs, etc., interfere with performance without people being aware of the extent of the damage. Or the place of work may need redesigning to take account of safety hazards; people have reported tremendous improvements in productivity, and the salvation of poor performance, after an office clean-out that took the typewriters down from the tops of cupboards, picked up the leads snaking across the floor, etc. People organise themselves so as to avoid safety hazards such as these, and this often interferes with doing the work efficiently. Where you have a poor performer with a high accident rate, look to see if changing the job environment or physical circumstances might improve things. Ask him if he has any suggestions –

make him responsible for carrying them out.

Look also for 'territory' problems. People need to feel that they have their own patch, a bit of space to call their own. Without this they usually become unsettled or aggressive or withdrawn, depending on their personality. Where you ask people to share things – share a desk, take turns on a machine, use a pool car, etc. – you deny them the right to call this their exclusive territory. There may be very good economic reasons why they should share – if your salesmen are on the road four days out of five there's no point in paying for each one of them to have an empty desk back at base – but if someone has no territory at all to call his own, or he has no sense of territory about the most important parts of his job (e.g. his tools and equipment) you may find performance problems occurring and need to look for a way of redesigning the job to give him a bit of turf to call his own. It could be as simple as a locked drawer of his own in the communal desk, or his own set of keys to the pool car. It could be that you let him establish some work territory at home. Some retail firms give their area managers an office at home, and allow them to employ a member of the family as a secretary. But he needs something to call his own, and a territory problem is often difficult for the sufferer to recognise and articulate, so you need to be doubly watchful in your diagnosis.

'Horizontal' job redesign

In a 'horizontal' job redesign you change the job so as to include (usually) more responsibilities on the same level as the existing job. The best example of a horizontal redesign is the change from assembly line to batch production, though this involves the whole team rather than just the individual poor performer. Other examples include giving the person responsibility for checking his own work as well as doing it; giving salesmen responsibility for collecting their own debts; enlarging or contracting the range of products a salesman is expected to sell; or giving the management trainer permission to operate in the field as well as in the classroom.

When would you use horizontal job redesign? It is most successful in the following circumstances:

1. *Adding interest and variety*. Just doing one small part of a

big process can be very boring indeed. It is sometimes said that the worker likes the boring job, because it permits him time to daydream about more interesting (non-work) subjects; we suspect that this may be true in some cases but not nearly as many as people would like to believe, and that many clerical and assembly-line jobs would be improved if they could be given a little more interest and variety.

2. *Creating a change of pace.* Working at a constant pace, be it fast or slow, is more stressful than working at a varied pace. If there is a single lesson to be learned in the management of stress at work it is this: *vary the pace* of your work. If people have the opportunity not merely to work at a variety of paces, but also have control over their pace of work so they can decide for themselves whether to work flat-out or to take their time, much of the stress they experience is eliminated. So job redesign can help if as part of the redesign more management of the pace of work is put into the hands of the poor performer – always assuming that he knows the standards expected of him and is not tempted to see this as a licence for slacking.

3. *Creating a sense of interdependence amongst the workforce.* A horizontal job redesign in the direction of batch production makes it clear to people how much they depend on each other, how their small mistakes cause big trouble for someone else, and how the other people are only human too. This brings into action the force of peer group pressure, which, as we illustrate in Chapter 15, is one of the most powerful forces a manager can bring to bear on the poor performer.

4. *Closing a feedback loop.* It's easy to perform badly if you never see the results of your actions. If your salesman gets a lot of returns or bad debts because he pressurises people into buying, then a good way of getting his performance to improve is to give him the responsibility for dealing with returns and bad debts – not just as a charge against his commission at the end of the month, but make him go and collect the returned equipment or ask for the bad debt to be paid off. Only when his job includes responsibility for the consequences of his own actions can he reasonably be expected to improve his performance. And the same argument applies wherever someone else is charged with dealing

with the aftermath of the poor performer's job. One sales organisation in the USA has a Vice-President for Objection Handling. Salesmen should have the kind of job description and training that makes them elicit fewer objections in the first place and deal with them themselves. If you have a customer complaints division, is this not encouraging people to perform badly in other parts of the organisation in the knowledge that some harassed body elsewhere will clear up their mess for them? Job redesign to bring people into closer contact with the consequences of their own actions will help your poor performer.

This kind of horizontal job redesign, where people in effect swap job responsibilities amongst themselves until as a group they are working well, is often made necessary by a previous job design that did not take into account the fact that people differ from machines. An assignment of tasks that might make economic sense if the jobs were all done by robots sometimes does not make sense if the jobs are to be done by people. The classic study which showed the sober truth of this assertion was done over twenty-five years ago, when the National Coal Board changed over to the 'longwall' method of getting coal. Previously people had worked in shifts (three shifts every twenty-four hours) and each group of miners in the shift had responsibility for getting the coal – cutting, blasting, putting up their own props, clearing away. The change to the longwall system – a change that involved millions of pounds' worth of equipment and a big change in working practice – meant that in general one team was given responsibility for moving the face forward, one team had responsibility for getting the coal, and the third responsibility for clearing away. Almost immediately the absenteeism rate went up and other indicators of morale went down, and a team was called in to investigate. They found that the change to the new system took away people's feeling of responsibility for their own work, and their feeling of teamwork. If at the end of the shift they had not finished all their work, or cleared up properly, it was the following shift who would have to cope. Under the previous arrangement they had to do it all for themselves or no-one else did it for them; now they could skimp the job, and not be faced directly with the consequences themselves. It was of course particularly tempting to do this when the previous shift had left work for you to clear up yourself. So a vicious circle developed, and the quality of work plummeted.

The interesting thing about this story is that people often react as if the miners were being somehow irrational or blameworthy. The feeling is that people should be able to cope in jobs which have been made uncongenial or frustrating by the introduction of new equipment or working practices. If the equipment is expensive then of course there is an element of self-justification involved. Yet sooner or later people must surely realise that it is better to plan not to give people the kind of job where they get no sense of completion, no sense of continuity, no control over their own pace of working – because all the evidence is that you can no more expect people to behave well when these things are lacking than you can expect concrete to perform well under tension or steel to perform well under compression.

However, widespread unrealistic attitudes mean that you may have difficulty persuading other people that this approach to poor performance is the best solution for the particular circumstances and not a compromise.

'Vertical' job redesign

In this approach to job redesign, responsibilities from levels above and below that of the jobholder are added to his existing ones. Usually this is done to meet objectives similar to those for horizontal redesign, with the addition of the opportunity to plan one's work. The most common kinds of vertical job redesign include more responsibility for planning the work, or more responsibility for presenting it to one's superiors in the organisation. Thus instead of the manager setting a detailed timetable, he just says what needs to be done by when and leaves it to the individual to decide how to schedule the work. Or instead of the manager getting the individual to put together a case which the manager then puts to his boss, the individual has responsibility for making the case himself.

Vertical job redesign is a special case of delegation, if you like to look at it in this way. It is a more permanent form of delegation, but it does not take away from the manager the ultimate responsibility for guidance on standards and the overall conduct of the work.

In practice all kinds of job redesign often take place at the same time, and the only reason the manager needs to make distinctions is to keep his records straight with the job evaluation people.

Job redesign and job enrichment is a fairly well-researched method of improving poor performance. A few years ago it seemed as if it were advocated as the only panacea for such cases. Research now indicates that its usefulness is confined to certain types of job problem:

1. White-collar workers benefit from job redesign programmes more than blue-collar workers, especially blue-collar non-assembly line jobs. In particular where you are working on the very borderline of employment – employing people with very few skills, employed for their muscle alone – job redesign is unlikely to help. The extra responsibility may take the job beyond the reach of the employees.
2. Where quality of work is the problem rather than quantity of work, job redesign is more likely to help. Job redesign is best regarded as a way of getting people to do things better, rather than to do more things. However, more managers need to press the *better* button than to press the *more* button – nonetheless, be careful about your expectations.
3. Problems of absenteeism or turnover are likely to benefit from job redesign programmes. The improved job interest and sense of responsibility and completion makes the job more attractive, lengthens the learning curve, and provides variety – all factors in attracting and retaining staff.

If you contemplate a job redesign programme it is tactically a good idea to involve the poor performer in the redesign even if you know yourself what needs to be done. The more of himself there is invested in the solution – the more he has had to think and work hard about it – the more likely it is that he will want to make it work. Use it when you believe the skills and motivation are there, but the job content makes it difficult for the poor performer to allow his motivation full rein, or the demands of the job frustrate his skills.

14 If you must reorganise . . .

This book is about improving the performance of people one at a time, while reorganisation is about groups. But we can't resist a brief word about reorganisation, because we have seen so many managers put blind faith in the prospects of a reorganisation to improve someone's performance only to find that nothing happens or the problem is worse. Indeed, we suspect that at least one good book could be written about the consequences of disastrous reorganisations – and most of the reorganisations that have any noticeable consequences at all have disastrous ones – if only top managers could overcome their natural reluctance to speak out about the 'Emperor's new organisation chart' and their resulting nakedness.

Reorganisation will not compensate for a lack of talent in the organisation. It merely spreads the existing talent differently. It's like the housewife who turns her sheets sides to middle; she's made the centre uncomfortable and pushed the bits that are wearing thin towards the outside, but she hasn't added any new material. Reorganisations need more careful support and planning than they usually get; and they are often introduced as the first resort, when they should in fact be the last.

The main reason for this is that structure does not cause function, it reflects it; and this is especially true in an existing organisation. The force of inertia stands in the way of any reorganisation. For instance, staff know that if they want some spares in a hurry, the thing to do is to sweet-talk Jim in the stores; then, with reorganisation Jim is re-christened the Spares Inventory Officer and told to give you a docket to fill out before you get your spares, and a new collection of channels to go through; you and Jim are going to find it in your joint interests to circumvent this new system and go back to the old way of doing things. The problem is that, while if you were designing a new organisation from scratch it might be a good idea to call Jim the Spares Inventory Officer and start him off with a whole new pile of dockets, you're not designing a new one, but tinkering with an old one; and most reorganisation plans are sadly lacking in ideas on how to get from here to there. Indeed when the vogue for reorganisation was at its height, some consultants made a selling point of the way they would recommend new structures, but not get involved in the implementation thereof. It is a good principle not to engage in battles you can't win; this seemed to be a case of engaging clients in a battle which they could not win.

It follows from the argument that structure reflects function rather than causing it that there may be a case for reorganising to formalise a state of affairs that has already come about. As organisations grow and change, lines of influence alter; sometimes a formal reordering of lines of command makes it easier to do what needs to be done. About any proposed reorganisation, therefore, one should ask: 'Is it a positive response to what people are already doing and asking for?' and 'Will it simplify present ways of getting things done?' and 'Will it enable us to give better service and meet our profit targets?' The last point is probably the most important, and the one easiest forgotten; look at the way most people approach the business of reorganisation, and you see that the poor customers and suppliers are the last people considered. If you deal with a small number of large organisations which are themselves organised in a certain structure, it may be to your advantage to mimic their structure in your own organisation so as to facilitate negotiation. If your customers find they are called on by a variety of salesmen each dedicated to pushing his own product at the expense of addressing the customer's unique needs, maybe it's time to reorganise so that the customer's life is made easier. This kind of reorganisation – the kind that makes it easier for the customer to buy from you, so much easier that the customers actually *notice* it – may have a marginal effect on the performance of some of your people if they had previously been prevented by the organisation from giving good customer service.

But in practice most reorganisations are not conducted for this purpose. They are conducted out of a desire for tidiness, control, change, or a spurious compatibility with the rest of the organisation. The *tidiness* motive usually finds expression in the design of hierarchies. Despite all the evidence that you don't always need a hierarchy to get things done, the tidiness freaks can't stand seeing teams the 'wrong' size, reporting relationships proliferating, absence of job descriptions (all properly evaluated), designated deputies, overlapping territories, and all the other housekeeping offences that people commit if they're in a hurry. So they tidy things up, draw lines on charts, put in control systems, etc. All organisations go through this crisis once they get past the early pioneering stage; and like any crisis, it contains many opportunities for fatal mistakes. Given half a chance, the tidiness freaks will tidy the soul out of the organisation, and in so doing will build for themselves an unchallengeable position. They usually build this by getting and keeping secret the information that other people would love to have. It's no coincidence that personnel departments often perpetrate these 'tidy' reorganisations, often for departmental rather than business reasons ('We must have a job evaluation scheme . . . a performance review scheme . . . rigidly defined merit pay . . .'), and in the course of implementation they get to know all the important information about the people in the organisation – which they then proceed to keep to themselves.

Then there's the reorganisation brought about to satisfy need for control. Like any human motivation, the need for control can be a good thing or a bad thing; it's generally agreed to be a good thing to know where the four million pounds you spent last year on computers actually went, and where you would need to start looking to find them (an actual problem for one UK firm), whereas control because you can't stand uncertainty is perhaps a less commendable motive. The problem with 'control' reorganisations is that they often change reporting relationships but don't support the change in relationships with adequate briefing and training. If things are so badly out of control that you really don't know where the money's going, you probably need shorter and better-defined reporting relationships and limits of authority. But the managers who let things get into this state need some education about how to make the new structure work for them – what areas to tell their people to report about, what questions to ask to detect problems early, etc. By itself the reorganisation is unlikely to do the job – a point to bear in mind if you hope that such a reorganisation will help a poorly-performing manager get back into control.

Of course, 'control' reorganisations can easily go too far. We have seen people seriously propose to reorganise good working relationships merely to let the personnel department have a smaller variety of appraisal forms to monitor. Reorganising the field to make head office's job easier is a common pastime, and should be avoided; the people in head office should be big and brave enough to cope with the kind of uncertainty that the average production manager lives with for most of his working life.

People also reorganise for variety's sake. They might phrase it differently, but that's their motive. We used to know a couple of organisations where it was rare for a manager actually to have to manage to the budget he'd drawn up, because jobs changed so frequently. After a few 'variety' reorganisations people get the message that there's no point trying too hard to do your job, as you'll just get on top of it and they'll change it; cynicism sets in remarkably fast. And on top of the deadening effect of the 'variety' reorganisations often comes an additional demotivator: for it is in these firms that the news gets around that you stand more chance of promotion by doing well out of a reorganisation than by working hard or acquiring new skills. It is in these organisations that one most often hears managers express the hope that their poor performers will improve as a result of the reorganisation; and it is here that their hopes are most regularly dashed.

People sometimes reorganise because they have just taken over a new company and they want the new acquisition run and managed in exactly the same way as the old one. Never mind if the two firms do entirely different things, work to different time-scales, address different markets, need a totally different risk-taking strategy. Out goes the old system; in goes the new; and in a matter of weeks chaos results. On a good day, the new owners will see this chaos as proof of why the new acquisition was doing so badly that they could take it over so effortlessly; and will congratulate themselves on their foresight in bringing in professional management systems where they were so sadly lacking.

What are we saying? Can the manager with a poor performer place any trust in reorganisation as a way of helping him with his problems? Well, not a lot; but here are some guidelines to getting the best out of a reorganisation if you want to improve someone's performance:

1. Try everything else first. After all, you're interested in *how* he does his job, not in where the job fits in to the rest of the organisation. Everyone will always grumble that he could do his job better if only someone over in another department did *his* job better – this is no compelling reason to reorganise. Maybe you need to get the two people together to discuss how they see each other. Maybe you need to get your poor performer trained in the skills necessary to cope with the other person. Maybe he doesn't see it as his job to have to cope with the other person, and you have to counsel him and agree what his job actually is.

Many managers have a psychological block about accepting this advice. The reason is a simple one – pride. Reorganisations are usually undertaken after seeking outside advice, or using a team of experts from head office. So if the reorganisation doesn't work, and the poor performance doesn't improve, it's easy to blame the people who recommended it. It's psychologically much more risky for the manager to say: 'No, this is my problem, and I have to solve it using my own resources.' Risky it may be, but safer in the long run.

2. *Ask for a diary.* If you have any say at all in the commissioning of a reorganisation, get the people working on it to project sample three-month diaries for some of the key people whose jobs they want to change. Get them to look at the number of functions these people will have to represent or co-ordinate, and then extrapolate to the number of meetings this will involve. Be realistic about the meetings – where will they be held and how much travelling time will they take up? How many reports will they have to read and sign off? How many budgets will they have to go through? How soon, therefore, will they be able to respond? How long will work take to get through the system? One thing reorganisations never do is project the workload they are imposing on people to see what it will look like in practice – how long it will take a manager on the ground to get approval for special expenditure, how many meetings a week people will have to be involved in, how much reading people are expected to do, etc. If the reorganisation team protest that this estimate can't be done, fire them. You wouldn't buy a car that had been designed but not tested, would you? If they do give you estimates, double them for safety, and then ask yourself whether your poor performer will be helped or hindered by the new pattern of activity. If he'll be hindered, try to get the reorganisation changed; if he'll be helped, start to prepare him to take advantage of the

new position by appropriate counselling and training.

3. Ask for the benefits. You need to know how the reorganisation will benefit the people you are responsible for – with particular emphasis on the poor performer. General benefits to the organisation as a whole are interesting, but not as relevant as benefits to the individual people. You need to ask this question (a) to help the reorganisation team stay in touch with the realities, and (b) to help you sell the reorganisation to your people.

4. Brief and train your people. There is no substitute for a personal briefing from the manager when people are told about a reorganisation. Look on the briefing exercise as a sales task; you have to sell the new type of organisation to your people. First, therefore, you must establish *needs* – what are the problems they experience in the present way of working, and do they hurt enough (or can you make them hurt enough) for them actively to desire a solution? Next you have to sell the benefits of the reorganisation, explaining how the new working practices will meet their needs for change. The wrong way to present a reorganisation – like any other product – is by describing its history and features without relating them to previously established needs.

You may need to offer training to cope with the reorganised jobs. Sometimes the training required is very simple – just explaining to people the purpose of any new forms they might have to fill in, or taking them to see the people they will have to liaise with. But if your reorganisation involves, say, putting people into contact with the customer who have never had to do this before, you must support this with good training – perferably on-the-job training – or risk upsetting the customers. If your reorganisation brings people into contact with the computer for the first time on-the-job training will again be needed. With your poor performer, you need to take the time to work with him through the period of changeover to make sure he takes advantage of the new opportunities. The skills and procedures discussed in Chapter 11 will help here. Try to get him to see the change as an opportunity, a chance to start again with a clean sheet. Make sure he knows what standards you expect from him in the new job. Make sure he knows what the limits of his authority are, what matters he should refer to you and where he should take decisions on his own initiative.

5. Be quick. We know one company where parts of it hadn't finished implementing one reorganisation before the second one, initiated four years later, started up. Reorganisations should allow enough time for people to get used to the changeover, especially if new equipment is being phased in at the same time, but after that the quicker the process is completed, the better.

To summarise: be very sceptical about the degree to which reorganisation will help your poor performer. The best you can sensibly hope for is to create an opportunity for him to start afresh, and you both need to work to take advantage of this opportunity. Much more important, in most companies, is to be on your guard against the false promises which reorganisation freaks will try to bemuse you with. Treat their offerings with harsh scepticism. Ask yourself how many people you know who are performing better as a result of a reorganisation, and be surprised if you do better.

15 Using peer group pressure

Of all the remedies open to a manager trying to correct poor performance, peer group pressure is probably the most reliable force he can use. The work group can achieve changes in performance which the individual manager finds impossible to accomplish by his own direct efforts. Unfortunately, peer group pressure is difficult to arrange; it's not as easily visible as a training course or job redesign or a disciplinary interview, and it's difficult for the manager to claim as his own effort. Nonetheless, where your poor performer's problems are attitudinal/motivational, rather than a simple lack of knowledge or skill, it's worth trying to arrange for the group he works with to put their own pressures on him.

Why should peer group pressure be so powerful? One reason is that peer group evaluations are generally very accurate. If you take from people at the end of a training course estimates of one anothers' potential, these estimates are usually more accurate than those made by the trainer or even by trained senior line manager observers. (Knowing that this is the case, we have tried repeatedly to get peer group evaluations built in to our management assessment programmes, but British culture usually rejects the practice. In America the 'buddy rating' system is commonly used and found to be accurate.) It's difficult to fool your peers. They undergo the same experiences as you do. They feel the same pressures. They work to the same standards. They work for the same manager. While a manager or supervisor only sees a limited part of his people's behaviour at work, the peer group sees it all. Peer group pressure is powerful also because of the degree of interdependence between the members. You're all obviously on the same ship.

Sometimes peer group pressure is made more powerful by the way the work is structured, or the way the reward system operates. Group bonus systems encourage peer group pressure. So does the autonomous work group. Where everyone's performance will be held down if one member fails to perform to standard, the group will try to do something about it.

How can the manager get peer group pressure to work for him? There are formal and less formal ways of invoking peer group pressure. In either case, it's usually a good idea if the manager does not reveal to the people concerned that this is what he is trying to do. It's likely that they will feel manipulated, especially if he uses jargon phrases like 'I'm going to use peer group pressure on you, Bill, it's the only thing left'. The manager must use all his art to create a situation where the work group feel that they must take responsibility for getting the poor performer to change, and they must feel afterwards that they take most of the credit. The manager must merely facilitate this happening.

Informal ways of using peer group pressure

Ask his mate to help him. Ask one of the more senior group members to help the poor performer. The helper must be given a specific brief: 'Bill seems to be having a bit of trouble making appointments. I've asked him if he won't mind your coming out with him next week to see if you can spot where the trouble lies and give him some tips on how to do a bit better.' 'Could you help Bill pull his month-end figures round?' is a much less useful way of asking for help. The helper needs to be reassured that his own job responsibilities will not suffer while he devotes some time and effort to helping Bill. He also needs briefing to look for behaviour, not personal qualities; and to give feedback as soon as possible after the event.

Sometimes you can enlist the helper's assistance as part of a conspiracy. 'I don't want to send him on a Head Office course, there isn't time and anyway he'd only come back with his head crammed full of theory. Can you spare the time to help him learn on the job?'

Be sure to keep in touch with the appointed helper to see how things are going and to give encouragement. The helper may expect miracles and need your counsel to stay patient; changes do not happen overnight, people do not instantly acquire new skill even when they have been shown the right way to do it. The helper needs your counsel to take things one step at a time, to have patience, to have the self-control not to ask the poor performer to admit that he's been helped.

Ask him to help his mate. Many poor performers have been

improved by being given responsibility for helping one of their mates. In showing a new arrival round the place, for example, your poor performer may get a renewal of the old pride in his work. The thought that you trust him enough to give him the task of helping someone else may bring him round. There is a fine judgement here. A really dyed-in-the-wool old cur-mudgeon is not the right person to choose for showing a new-comer the ropes; more likely he'll scare the novice away or gleefully induct him into some old bad habits. But the younger poor performer, of whom you would say 'His heart's in the right place, it's just a question of organising him right', is likely to be helped by being given such a task.

If you ask the poor performer to help someone else, you can use the chance subtly to clarify standards and methods with him. This is a good way of training by stealth. You can say that although you are fairly sure he knows what needs to be done, the opportunity of helping someone else means that you should both be clear beyond doubt about the standards and skills which the job involves.

Make group pay or esteem depend on group performance. If you have a merit payment system, or a commission system, there are often problems about the fair assignment of bonuses, on the grounds that everyone in the office contributes by answering telephone calls, lending a hand, keeping the administration going, etc. Some organisations try to overcome these natural feelings by assigning a group bonus – given to the team as a whole – instead of or in addition to the individual bonus. Here is another opportunity to use peer group pressure to improve the poor performer, for if the group feel that he will bring their bonus down they will try to take action.

The trick here is to make the reward sufficiently tempting for the group to bring pressure, but not so tempting that they try to ditch him. And you do need to check that the deficiency is not something you as a manager could do something obvious and direct about, like offering formal training. If he has the basic skills and abilities, but just needs persuading to improve his standards, then the group are likely to exert effective pressure on him. By 'effective pressure' we don't mean that they'll send the heavies in; most frequently the group pressure starts with timekeeping and good housekeeping, and all they need to do is to police their own breaks, ask him whether he's really going to go home leaving his work station in such a mess, and so on. Group pay or bonus is one effective way of bringing pressure to bear; even without merit pay, management actions that obviously praise the work group as a work group rather than as individuals can have similar effects. The competitive charts that one sees on factory floors, sales offices, etc., have their own effect even when they are not backed up by money.

Make him part of an autonomous work group. Give a group of people responsibility for organising their own work, and they will make sure that poor performers don't lag behind. This is the same pressure as the self-imposed limits on output that management often grumbles about; turned on itself this same pressure is responsible for groups wanting to keep work up to a certain quality and standard, and they will usually act to bring round anyone who is not being helpful. In the present day the best-known autonomous work groups are part of the Volvo experiment in Sweden, though small car manufacturing has worked on the Volvo pattern for many years, and teams of professionals (e.g. lawyers, doctors, architects) have worked in small autonomous groups policing their own standards for years. Typically the autonomous work group sets higher quality standards and is more concerned about consistent achievement of quality than quantity. If you want very fast production the assembly line is still your best bet, and if you want a trouble-free assembly line you had better automate it. If in your business you can sacrifice quantity for quality an autonomous work group may be part of the answer for bringing peer group pressure to bear on the poor performer.

The autonomous work group management asks for a given amount of work to be done, but leaves it up to the group how they plan and carry out the work. Standard-setting may be a joint activity with management, or the group may do it alone. If you follow the thoughts of a poor performer through this process you may come to understand why peer group pressure is so powerful. First, they have to clarify standards together. In clarifying his standards with management, the poor performer may well be thinking: 'What's the least I can get away with doing?' but with his working colleagues he is more likely to be anxious to please, more likely to accept the higher standards they propose for him.

Then they have to agree how to share the work. It will be

obvious to him if anyone else is trying to shirk responsibilities and put more work on the rest of the team. He will probably feel resentful of this. When it comes to his turn, he will know that the rest of the group are anxious to make sure that he does his share – and that will be difficult to say No to.

Once work starts, it's the experience of shared failure and success that gives peer group pressure its great force. It's difficult not to pull your weight when you know that with one more extra bit of effort the whole team could meet its target. When you have together shared the pleasure of having the work go well, the frustrations of having it go badly, the annoyance at sheer bad luck for one of your colleagues, it's difficult not to get drawn in and want to do well.

This is how peer group pressure works. Reinforce it with peer group payment schemes or league tables if you like. The key thing is to get people feeling that they as a group are responsible for their own work standards and methods, and they will take on responsibility for dealing with the demotivated performer.

Of course, it's difficult to apply peer group pressure if your peer group is scattered all over the country. It doesn't work anything like as well if the group only meets once a week. And there are some people who are so consistently anti-joining that they don't respond to pressure. But if you can find ways of increasing the workers' sense of interdependence the chances are you have a good vehicle for dealing with many performance problems.

Formal ways of using peer group pressure

In one or two organisations a deliberate attempt has been made to use peer group pressure to improve performance all round and take specific action with poor performers. These formal methods look so promising that we shall report them briefly here, using one large organisation as the model.

In this model organisation, which depends on getting revenue from the public, many customer contact staff did not see it as their job to help the public or to try to sell the firm's services. The staff are spread over depots all over the country. Most of the staff are old and unskilled and long for the days when life was less complicated, people knew exactly what they wanted, had the right change ready, and you needn't say a word to the

customers from morning till night. Market surveys had identified an enormous potential revenue which was being lost,
partly because of the actions of these depot staff. While some of
the staff believed that their job was to help the customers and to
sell, others did not; clearly a poor performance problem on a
massive scale. We were asked to look at the problem – initially it
was diagnosed as a sales training problem for which we were to
design a sales training course. On closer examination we came to
believe that while there were some specific sales skills lacking –
staff had never been trained to deal with people over the telephone, for example – the problems were largely to do with
attitudes. While each depot could benefit from improvement in
skill, the skills would be of little use without the attitudes necessary to put the skills in practice. And we discovered that in each
depot there lurked one or two poor performers, people whose
attitude was acknowledged to be so bad that you exposed them
to the public at your own risk, and mostly tried to keep them
busy on clerical work at the back of the store.

We decided that if we were to change the attitudes of our poor
performers then peer group pressure was our only answer, and
we had to apply it in the guise of a training course. So we
designed a year-long training course – we knew that if you want
lasting changes in attitude you must bring them about slowly but
surely. The evangelical conversions look very pretty when you
see the feet rushing towards the pulpit, but six weeks later over
half their owners will be back sinning for dear life. Our training
course was administered by three trainers recruited from inside
the organisation; they had themselves all done the job of the
people they were training. Each trainer had a certain number of
depots, and he spent one day per week at each depot. During the
day he took the staff off the job in small groups, for half an hour
at a time, for a short training session. Each training session
covered one aspect of sales skills (e.g. establishing customer
needs, giving information over the telephone, etc.) or product
knowledge. The sessions were designed in advance, and at the
end of each session the trainees were given a summary sheet of
notes which they put into a manual which eventually became
their 'sales skills manual'. The training programme started in
September. One of the things we had been careful to warn the
trainers about when they applied for the job was that there
would be no breakthroughs for six months or more, and that

there would be many a wet Thursday in winter when they would go home having encountered nothing but antagonism and had nobody to talk to. We had to be careful to select trainers with the strength of character to cope with these pressures.

At the beginning, the staff were very sceptical indeed. For most of them this was the first training they had ever received since joining the organisation, and the trainers got a barrage of complaints about what was wrong. The poor performers – the *really* poor performers – either made excuses to stay away, or attended and produced streams of objections. It was not until February that some of them started to come round; then we began to hear from the trainers that people who had previously stayed away had started to attend, or that the rest of the group were telling the grumblers to shut up and listen because the trainer had something useful to say.

Eventually when we conducted a post-course attitude survey we found a tremendous shift in attitude had taken place, mostly in the last six months; whereas at the start of the training only about 25 per cent of the staff had agreed that they liked selling and their job was to sell, now about 85 per cent said that they liked selling, they believed that their job was to sell, they liked asking customers questions, they could see the customers' point of view, etc. As far as we could tell, these improvements in staff attitude were also correlated with improvements in the public perception of their helpfulness, and with increased revenue. The programme was a conscious effort to use peer group pressure to change staff attitudes and correct poor performers. Analysis of why it succeeded leads us to believe that the following factors were responsible:

1. The trainers were 'peers' in the sense that they themselves had recently done the jobs they were asking people to do better. Indeed, there were some times of crisis when the trainers stopped training, rolled their sleeves up, and helped man the staff positions. Had we used outside trainers, or trainers from senior management positions, the training would not have worked as well. (We know, because we were able to compare our training using peer-trainers with the same training programme administered in a different part of the organisation by 'expert' trainers.)
2. We consciously set ourselves limited objectives – one skill

at a time rather than the swamping evangelical conversion. By chipping away at the undesirable attitudes we achieved a longer-lasting change than if we had gone for a head-on confrontation. Each time, we only asked people to do one small thing differently. Each time, we set limited objectives and low expectations.

3. We took the training to the troops on the ground. This was much more valuable than ever we had expected it to be. Normally in a classroom training course people grumble: 'It's OK for you to say it here, but you haven't actually been to our depot and seen what it was like last week when the pipes burst.' They no longer had this excuse. If conditions were bad or there were particular local problems, the trainer experienced them as well as the trainees. No longer could they protest that he was offering them 'only theory'; many a time they actually left the 'classroom' and the trainer showed them how to put the theory into practice in a real situation.

4. They had some early successes. In the first few modules of the training programme we included the development of some skills which would make life easier for the trainees, although they did not think so at first. For instance, we taught them more about how to ask their customers' questions. Usually they shied away from doing this, on the grounds that getting into a conversation with a customer would hold them up and prevent them from getting on with other things or attending to fresh customers. Some of the more adventurous were persuaded to try our advice, and they found that if they asked the customers questions they could deal with the customers more quickly and with fewer return queries, while at the same time the customers felt that the staff were taking a personal interest in them. It only needed a couple of people at each depot to report that the trainers actually had some good ideas and were talking sense for the rest of the group to become less sceptical. When the existing poor performers saw that their mates who followed our advice were doing the job faster and with less trouble, they started to attend and in some cases asked for catch-up sessions.

5. We responded quickly to business changes. Once we had the regular cycle established of the trainer visiting each depot once a week, we could inject new training modules to respond to business changes. The firm announced two important new

products while the training was in progress, and in both cases we had training modules and product briefing material ready for the trainer to use in the week the announcement was made. This brought us a lot of credit, as normally information about new products took a long time to filter down to the shopfloor.

6. We were a visible token of management support. In this firm very little training had been done previously; such training as was done was done by 'instructors' who followed rigid lecture patterns; and all training was known to include assessments of the trainees at the end. In this austere atmosphere we would have got nowhere if we had tried to improve performance by classroom training. Taking the training to the troops on the ground was a visible sign that we were trying to do something new, and trying to communicate a change of management style. The trainers came from the head office, normally a remote place associated in people's minds with job interviews, formal reprimands, and accountancy; but these trainers were accessible, normal human chaps – quite different from the head office stereotype. The rate at which people offered suggestions started to go up; when some of the suggestions were acted on the rate of silly suggestions dropped and some people put forward really good ideas which they had been scared of offering previously.

7. We offered praise. When the trainers saw someone doing a job well, they actually said Well done and Thank you. These were words not often used in this organisation. They made a difference. People began to see that good performance would be noticed as well as poor performance.

As a result of this programme we know that it is possible to organise peer group pressure to change attitudes and performance at work. We know that the change has lasted, though it will need support now from the supervisors if the impetus is not to be lost. We know from experience in two further organisations where similar programmes are going on that this is not an isolated instance. It's not quick; it takes time and patience and trust that it will eventually work. In the firm reported above, we found that local management support was a factor in how successful we were; there were a couple of depots where the manager was hostile and we were less successful. We also found that one depot with a staggeringly high labour turnover should not have taken part in the scheme, though it was included for the sake of consistency; it would have been better to spend the money trying to solve the labour turnover problem, which was clearly caused by appalling selection and induction methods.

Using peer group pressure like this is a little like dissolving medicine in a spoonful of sugar. You infiltrate into the groups on an acceptable and valid pretext – like sales skill training, product knowledge training, new technology briefing – a trained person whom the group will regard as a peer. Create a space for him to get the work group together on a regular basis. When the group is together he follows a plan of training, briefing, or discussion, around a given topic, and tries to draw the problem performers into his net – or to get the rest of the group to pull them in. By slow but sure use of carrot and stick he gets the problem performers attending, interested, trying out the new methods. Then by offering praise and support to the whole group he tries to consolidate the problem performers' change of heart.

Formally or informally, then, you can use peer group pressure on your poor performer. Before you try to arrange this, check to make sure that the poor performance is not caused by lack of skills and abilities – peer group pressure will not compensate for a lack of these, and may in fact make the problem worse. Check too that the peer group you are thinking of using is in fact the peer group he will recognise – he's more likely to see as his peer group the people he interacts with on a daily basis, rather than the people who are nominally on his level on the organisation chart but physically fifty miles away. Check also that his relationship with the peer group is such that they can put pressure on him, that he does want their esteem and approval. If he's a solitary PhD grumbling that he never gets any challenging work, and you want to mobilise the rest of the department who are all HND standard, you may find that he actually doesn't see them as part of the solution, but as part of the problem.

Once you have done this initial checking, your part as the manager is to arrange things so that peer group pressure comes into play; you have to clear the channels, so to speak, along which it will flow. The suggestions earlier in this chapter should give you some ideas about the kind of channel to create. After that, your own direct influence should not be very visible, or the advantage of using peer group pressure may disappear. Be careful that you don't let on about what you're going to do; your own boss and your expert staff adviser should be able to help, but don't threaten the poor performer with: 'If you don't improve I'm going to put peer group pressure on you,' because that way he'll only dig his heels in out of sheer stubbornness. And when the changes start to come about, be careful to give the group credit for its improvement, and don't point out to them how carefully you yourself cleared the channels and prepared the ground for the improvement to take place. People don't like to be told that they are predictable.

16 Professional counselling

There are occasions where the manager of a poor performer believes that he needs to arrange counselling for his poor performer but feels that the nature of the problem takes it outside the remit of an 'amateur' counsellor. In this chapter we review the circumstances which might lead you to use a professional counsellor, the different counselling services available, and some of the cautions to heed when using these outsiders.

When to use outside counsellors

The kind of indicators you would look for here are: strong emotional or attitudinal problems interfering with performance or with the success of your own counselling efforts; medical problems; and money problems. Outside counselling is of less use where the problems are skill or knowledge deficiency, lack of proper training, poor working conditions, or an organisation not supportive of good work.

You are likely to detect the strong emotional or attitudinal problems during your early investigations and counselling interviews. If the poor performer expresses a lot of hostility towards you or the firm as a whole; if he makes a great many statements of why it is difficult for him to change and appears actively not to want a solution no matter how hard you try to impress upon him the need for one; if he appears apathetic or uninterested no matter how hard you try; if you know that the rest of the work force dislike him, are jealous of him, cut him out of their activities – then you may have a problem so deep that you need outside help.

Often the non-verbal signals someone gives out in a counselling interview are helpful in detecting the extent of the difficulty. It is much easier to lie with your words than with your whole body. If someone laughs nervously while denying there is any problem you may want to investigate further before you actually believe him. Other non-verbal signals include: shifting the feet a lot, playing with keys, small change, fingers; sudden stiffness or actions taken to keep the body from giving things away, like tight folding of the arms and anchoring the legs.

Medical problems are likely to be more easily admissable, except for the range of minor personal miseries that most people are reluctant to talk about. Don't forget that even in these supposedly enlightened times, women may find it easier to discuss medical problems with women, and men with men. Some financial difficulties are easier to admit to than others. You as a manager should be alert for the kind of circumstances that can cause financial problems – the young marrieds going from two on two wages to three on one; the cessation of over-time payments on moving into management; the loss of opportunity to create overtime payments; bringing financial records onto computers with the loss of opportunities to fiddle; and so on. Your poor performer might not admit it if you asked 'Any money problems?' but might agree with you if you actually had something specific to suggest, like 'How are you managing now your wife's stopped working?'.

Specific money problems are associated with redundancy and the fear of redundancy. If you have made some people redundant, in the rest of the work-force some people may perform better, but for others the extra motivation induced by the need to avoid redundancy could, paradoxically, lead to poorer performance. Good financial counselling can lessen the blow of redundancy to a remarkable degree, so if you embark on a redundancy programme it is worth publicising the efforts you have gone to to make sure that people get the best possible financial deal and the best possible financial advice.

What counselling is available?

There are many different kinds of outside counsellors for you to call on, directly or indirectly. Amongst the most commonly used are:

Medical doctors
Your firm may have its own doctors, or you may need to suggest to the problem performer that he sees his GP. More and more companies are using the medical screening and advisory services provided by the private health care organisations, for their executives and key workers. The advantages of such screening

are (a) that it is preventive, looking for trouble spots before they become life-threatening or work-disruptive, and (b) that it uses professional counsellors who have more time to spend with the individual than his GP may have. Some of the screening services have built-in questions about the work environment and the person's way of life, to detect possibly damaging stress factors before they become a serious problem.

It is a pity that the cost of this screening, even with reduction for corporate membership, is so high that most of the firms who use it regard it as something for senior executives only. Some of the canteen subsidy – which goes into making suet puddings cheaper – might be better spent on making medical screening accessible to the whole of the workforce. Then any poor performer suspected of having medical problems could be sent by his manager for a full check-up without the fears sometimes voiced that the local GP knows too little about the conditions the person works under and will not be sensitive in his recommendations to the realities of the patient's working life.

Of course, as soon as you advise your poor performer to seek medical advice you lose direct control of the data. The doctor works for his patient, and only with the patient's consent should he release medical data to outsiders. The exceptions are medical examinations on hiring, or medical examinations by the company doctor of someone whose extended sick leave requires that he be re-examined at regular intervals. But if you have established a helpful and supportive atmosphere with your poor performer you should not experience too much difficulty in getting him to share with you his doctor's advice.

Psychiatric help
Medical ethics dictate that a psychiatrist, like any other medical specialist, can only be approached on the referral of another doctor. If you suspect that your poor performer is in need of psychiatric help, therefore, your first route must be the same as getting medical help – to the GP, or to a screening service which will contact the GP for referral to a psychiatrist if he thinks it is necessary.

If the poor performer takes a work-related problem to a psychiatrist, it is helpful if the psychiatrist knows something about business. These are fairly rare birds. It is a particular problem for women workers with work-related problems, as most psychiatrists (and most GPs) assume still that women who present with stress or emotional problems owe their difficulties to family circumstances. Many women have complained that they are offered psycho-sexual counselling or family therapy for a work-related problem, and that they have difficulty getting their advisers to treat their work problems with the same degree of seriousness as they would treat a male presenting them with the same problem. How you actually go about finding a psychiatrist who understands the pressures of business and industry is, of course, a more difficult question, but the poor performer should not neglect to ask in case, by happy chance, he finds he has a choice.

Industrial chaplains

Quite a few companies use industrial chaplains as counsellors, not merely for overtly religious or spiritual problems. There are some industrial chaplains in full-time employment in heavily industrialised areas; in other areas a local firm may have an arrangement with the local parish priest that he comes in for a couple of days a month and is available as a good friend and honest broker for anyone who wants to talk.

We have seen some of these relationships working extraordinarily well. The chaplain obviously has no management axe to grind; he has been trained in professional counselling techniques; he has relationships with other professional helpers in the community like local doctors; he will have relationships outside work with some of the employees and managers; and if his is a long-term relationship with the firm he will know the organisation, as well as some or all of the managers in it. In some companies the relationship with the chaplain is so strong and useful that the chaplain is used to feed back the results from company attitude surveys and talk individually with anyone who reports himself in the attitude surveys to be discontented with his job.

Of course the problems in using an industrial chaplain are (a) finding one in the first place if you are not already in an area served by a full-time dedicated one, (b) getting him introduced into the firm and on a basis of trust with everyone around, as he is likely to be seen as a nosy parker while he is settling down, (c) giving him a remit without unnecessarily prescribing his field of activity, and (d) avoiding affronting people who have their own attitude to religion and do not want to have to negotiate with someone they see as having mainly proselytising ambitions. You can't suddenly call on the services of an industrial chaplain when you have a problem; he needs to have been around for a while beforehand, as part of the scenery in the same way that the nurse or the safety officer is part of the scenery. So the main problems come in deciding how you will get someone accepted and inducted so that he is there on call when he is needed.

Financial counsellors
As financial legislation gets more and more complicated more and more people could benefit from financial advice. Even the simple family with a mortgage, two children, and one income can find itself paying more tax than it need, or in difficulties when retirement approaches. People receiving state benefits may find themselves in several interlocking poverty traps. If you have tried to reduce people's tax liabilities by altering their benefits packages you may have effects which you did not foresee. For all these reasons, some firms have started to offer their employees personal financial counselling, either on request or as part of a deal on moving house, promotion, or change of status. Where personal financial counselling has been made available on a considerable scale inside the organisation the counsellors have sometimes been able to pay for themselves by noticing that with a change in compensation policy the firm could achieve the same benefits to its employees, or more benefits, with no increased total outlay. There was a small boom in the use of personal financial counsellors in the UK when government regulations limited the scope for wage increases – some companies took the view that if they could not pay their employees any more they would at least see to it that their existing salaries were wisely spent. Financial counselling is often made available as part of a redundancy package. We believe that it could be made more widely available as a resource managers could use to help their poor performers who are worried about money.

You need to choose your counsellor carefully. Some will offer to do the counselling for a very small sum, or nothing at all. This may mean that they hope to make their money from recommending insurance policies, and in particular insurance policies that pay them a good commission. It is much better to choose a counsellor from a reputable company, and pay the company a fee for their professional services, having first assured yourself that the company do not see this as an opportunity for some paid marketing of costly financial packages. They should be prepared to advise on tax problems, state benefits, pension problems, etc., as well as mortgages and insurance policies.

Career and vocational guidance
Sometimes you may want to send your poor performer to someone who can advise him whether he has in fact chosen the right career for himself, and discuss his career management with him. You may find this necessary with younger poor performers, or with older people who are involved in redundancy or mid-career change. It's also something that many managers worry about in connection with their own children.

A good vocational guidance counsellor will probably use psychological tests and inventories to learn more about where the person's interests and aptitudes lie. It's important to test both of these: you need to know what the person *can* do, what he is good at (working with words, with figures, at detailed work, with mechanical objects, etc.) and also what he is *interested* in (meeting people, working with things, working outdoors, working under pressure, etc.). Two of the tests most commonly used on the general population are the Differential Aptitude Test (described in Chapter 3) and the Strong-Campbell Interest Inventory (for examining interests). The counsellor may add other tests to suit particular purposes, but be sure to ask (a) whether the tests have been validated for use in the country you are working in, and (b) where the validation figures have been published. If the counsellor cannot show you published validation data for the tests he is using, or if he uses no tests at all in this area where precision is all-important, show him the door. Do not accept 'assurances' like the one currently offered by a large UK firm of consultants who have been marketing an unvalidated test for a number of years; they say: 'Since our test is not intended for use as a selection instrument but merely as a way of collecting information for later discussion there is no need for validation studies to be performed.' This test, by the way, claims to measure twenty independent factors, each on a ten-point scale, by the use of ninety questions – a feat of measurement enviable in an exact science, were it possible, and one that should arouse extreme scepticism when claimed in the much less exact science of predicting human potential.

Having tested the person's interests and aptitudes the vocational counsellor should discuss with him the degree to which his present job uses his skills or makes demands on him which he is unable to fulfil or not interested in fulfilling. If they discover together a serious mismatch between skills and interests on the one hand, and the job content on the other, it falls to them to talk about other career options open. If you as the manager have the opportunity to brief the vocational counsellor first, you need to establish whether you want him to examine other jobs within your firm, or whether you are prepared to have the discussion range across all possible jobs – thus taking into account the possibility of the employee leaving the company altogether. If you would rather try to keep him with you, but perhaps in a different kind of job, then you may want to become personally involved in the feedback and counselling interviews, or get a member of the personnel department involved, because you are more likely to know the circumstances of your own firm. Together, you and the outside vocational counsellor could achieve a satisfactory result.

Other trained counsellors
There may well be other sources of counselling available to you. Some medium and large firms have one or two people in the central office whose job it is to counsel difficult employees, and have to this end had formal counselling training and belong to counselling organisations. It is important to make clear to the poor performer if you send him for counselling who the counsellor is working for – you or him, who will have access to any data generated and how, if at all, any report-back to yourself is to be conducted. These skilled internal counsellors, when we have seen them at work, perform an excellent service; our only worry is for their own career prospects, because the amount of information they gain is tremendous. It is therefore a post for an older person who is known to be staying in that post until retirement, or a younger person who sees his career permanently in these terms.

In some industries a network of advisers already exists, paid for by the industry association or the government. In the UK, for example, some industries replaced their Industry Training

Boards by voluntary equivalents, and there are trade associations and government-funded advisers for industries like agri-
culture. Europe and the United States make similar provisions
in some sectors. If you have access to a good independent
adviser it is like having a super consultant on tap, without you
hearing and tinkle of cash registers every half an hour. Again
you need to make it clear to all parties whom he is working for
and what he will do with his data – but with that proviso, if you
have access to a good independent adviser, use him.

Other consultants may offer counselling services also. A skilled consultant, particularly one who knows your firm through
regular association, can be very helpful. There are two things to
beware of here: first, that you do not get the type of consultant
who undertakes this kind of assignment in order to uncover
other problems which his firm is better equipped to cope with;
and secondly you need to be open with your poor performer
about the consultant's remit. We have ourselves been asked on
more than one occasion to interview staff on a pretext and then
report back to senior management on the ones who should be
sacked. And there was one firm of consultants who specialised
in undertaking meek-looking assignments (e.g. work studies)
and would then seek a special meeting with the managing director to tell him that they had uncovered disturbing evidence that
his managers were disloyal, and for a fee they would present him
with the full story. It should go without saying that secret agen-
das spell trouble and must be avoided at all costs.

Cautions in using outside counsellors

We will summarise here the cautions that have appeared
throughout this chapter – things you should take into consideration before using an outside counsellor to help your poor performer:

1. *Who is the client?* You must make it clear to everyone
concerned who the actual client is – is it to be the poor
performer himself, is it to be you as his manager, or will it be
some other part of your organisation like the personnel
department? This decision must then be taken into account in
deciding who receives reports, who has the responsibility for
reporting back, and who has the responsibility for taking
follow-up action.

2. *Who pays?* It is not uncommon for the company to pay, while stating that the prime client is the poor performer himself. All parties need to be clear about this, and the poor performer needs to know how much discretion he has in paying for help.
3. *Any preferred solutions should be made clear from the start.* By this we mean that if, for instance, you wish to limit the discussion between the two parties to what the poor performer can do in his present organisation, and to exclude the possibility of his leaving altogether, you should make sure that people know this at the outset. Similarly if you have policy constraints on the compensation package you can offer someone, the financial counsellor needs to know about this.
4. *The counsellor's power needs to be made clear to both parties.* If he is limited to advising the poor performer only, say so. If he could go on to talk to other people in the organisation about the problem, make sure that both parties know this. You do not want a situation where the poor performer believes that the counsellor will act as an advocate for him in higher places while the counsellor is in fact powerless to act.

Finally, bear in mind that you as a manager may learn some unpalatable things about yourself if the counsellor reports back to you in any form. Almost certainly the counsellor will uncover failings of management, as well as trying to treat the poor performer's own problems. In most cases where managers engage outside counsellors to help with their poor performers, the counsellors finish up doing two counselling interviews – one with the poor performer and one with his manager. Certainly the attitudinal or emotional problems – as opposed to the clearly financial or medical problems – by the time they have developed to the point of needing counselling require that both parties re-examine their attitudes. So don't expect a good counsellor to take the problem completely off your hands; don't be surprised if he wants to come and spend some time with you as part of the counselling process; and don't be surprised if he asks you to change the way you do things as part of the bargain he has arranged with your poor performer.

17 Training

You may decide that your poor performer needs formal off-the-job training. This could be the case if he lacks the necessary knowledge or skill to do the job properly and you believe the gap is small enough to be covered by adequately managed training. Large gaps in knowledge or skill may need different remedies. If your performer's problem lies more with his attitude or motivation, you must be especially circumspect about what training can do for you. Problems of attitude or motivation can be tackled by training sometimes, but it needs the long on-the-job type of training to give changes time to take place. A formal training course may help attitudes if you want to give the poor performer confidence that he can do something which he didn't believe he could – in that sense a training course could change attitudes. But where your problems lie in negative attitudes to the work or the work group, or badly organised motivation to work, you should consider other kinds of action first.

A good training course should give people ample opportunity to practise the new knowledge and skills, in a safe environment where it's OK to make mistakes. Your poor performer may be reluctant to change on the job because, bad though he believes his present performance to be, he feels that any change could only be to a less familiar and therefore worse way of doing things. On a good training course he will have the chance to try out new ways himself in the knowledge that nothing disastrous is likely to happen to the business.

There are three important provisos to bear in mind. The first is that you should not send your poor performer on a training course where the trainees get assessed as part of the course. Indeed, assessments as part of a training course are pretty well guaranteed to put everyone on their best behaviour and to make them indulge in 'coursemanship', whereas what you want is for people to try different kinds of behaviour. Recently we took part in a training programme where, unknown to us, the participants expected to be assessed as was normal on their organisation's training courses. On the afternoon of the second day we realised that this was their expectation, and made it clear that no assessment would be made by us. Immediately people started to experiment with the new skills which hitherto they had treated warily. Nobody can learn to do new things if at the same time he is being assessed to see whether he already knows them.

You must also bear in mind that the training is unlikely to work if the poor performer himself does not agree with it. So all the skills of persuading him that he has a serious problem and really wants a solution – skills outlined in Chapter 11 – must come into play here. It's no good saying, out of the blue, 'Harry, I'm sending you on a course' – you need to get his commitment to going. Certainly you should resist using compulsion to get him to the course. Managers sometimes feel like using compulsion when they think that the problem is too big for them to handle and that they can hand it over to the course trainer, who is by definition more skilful. But any trainer will tell you that the door to a man's mind can be locked from the inside, and there's no surer way to get him behind the barricades than to force him onto a training course against his will. Ideally your strategy of making him own the problem and want a solution will lead to him asking for your suggestions about a course. In the less-than-ideal case you'll both develop the idea together. But to tell him with no introductory questioning that you think a course is right for him is committing the error the bad salesman commits when he rings up and says 'I'd like to introduce you to our new patent dog-exercising system', with no attempt to make you feel a need that such a device could satisfy.

The third consideration in sending someone on a training course is the gap between your poor performer and the other people on the course. Sometimes managers say: 'Let's put him on a course with some really good performers so that he can see what life's all about when you're on top of your job.' It's a laudable intention, but you have to manage the gap carefully. Your poor performer must feel (a) that he would like to be like the good ones, (b) that he is capable of bridging the gap, and (c) that he can actually bridge the gap on the course or while he is still under its immediate influence. If the gap between himself and the others is too big, the odds are he will find some rationale for believing that they are so totally different from him that he could never bridge the gap. If the gap is significant but manageable, then he could respond to the challenge. This consideration often presents itself when it is suggested that the poor performer go on an outside course – 'put him up against the high-flyers from more professional organisations'. In order to see whether he is being offered a manageable challenge you must find out quite a lot about the other people who will be on the course, or the standard of acceptance for the course.

How to choose a training course

To choose a training course you need to write down clearly what the poor performer does now that you want changed, and what you want him to be able to do after the course. Keep this statement by you – you will need it to navigate your way through the jungle of literature that will soon engulf you. Publishers of course brochures (and we mean internal training departments as well as outside course organisers) have a number of sophisticated ways of making you lose contact with this specification. They give their courses fancy, catch-all titles that often include the latest buzz-word; they give long lists of course content that look like school prospectuses, without any notion of the standards or methods of teaching; they give long lists of all the other organisations who use their training courses, assuming that they only have to get one ICI executive along for half a day to claim that ICI sponsor or endorse their courses. No, what you need to know about is what will actually happen on the training course and whether it will meet your needs. Unless you are lucky and get one of the few good course brochures around, this means you will have to ring up the course organiser or go and see your training department. Here are some questions you should ask them:

1. *What teaching methods are used?* The things to beware of here are: over-dependence on lectures (people usually find an hour's lecture long enough, and the attention tends to wander more quickly after lunch); over-dependence on group discussions where the subject-matter really ought to be taught by an expert capable of overcoming the attention loss at the end of a lecture; lack of practice (many courses ask people to spend too long watching other people do things, and not enough time doing them themselves). The distinction to look for is between the kind of training course where it is safe to assume

that between them the trainees actually know most of the
right things to do and it's simply a matter of putting them into
work groups so that they teach each other, and on the other
hand the kind of course where the trainees come to be taught
by an expert and need to go into work groups to consolidate
and practise what they have actually learned.

2. *Can I see the notes?* Ask for a look at the course materials
that will be used. If your trainee is expected to make all his
own notes, ask if he is given any guidance in doing this. (We
favour a wordbook where the key issues to be covered on the
course are indicated by a series of questions, but the trainee is
free to note down what sticks in his mind.) Ask yourself
whether you are satisfied with the amount of notes or guidance that he will get on the course.

3. *How much practice will my trainee get on the course?* If he
is being asked to absorb new knowledge, he will want several
opportunities to try it out. Many courses give only one. Some
only give you the chance to watch other people try it out. The
same thing goes for skills – if he is going to the course to learn
new skills, he wants lots of opportunity to try these skills, not
just to watch other people trying them.

4. *What sort of feedback will he get on the course?* People
don't learn new skills without feedback. Feedback needs to be
planned as part of the training programme, and it needs to be
planned against some rational analytical model. It is not
'feedback' in the learning sense of the term if the course
consists of a series of group discussions at the end of which
people are invited to tell each other what they thought of their
performance, or the trainer gives an insight into this feelings.
The trainer needs an observation or marking schedule against
which to collect data relevant to the skills or knowledge under
development, so that he can feed back a reliable and thorough
picture.

5. *What qualifications does the trainer have?* This is a two-
part issue. First the trainer must actually be able to convince
you that he knows what he is talking about. Secondly he must
have the personal authority or style that commands the
respect of the trainees. It is often the qualifications of external
trainers which are used to make an impression on senior or
middle management, even though there are people inside the
firm who could do the job just as well.

6. *Are the case studies and exercises up-to-date?* It will upset your poor performer and make him lose faith in the training if he finds that he is expected to work with exercises that have not been changed for ten years, so that all the dates, figures, money amounts, and the legislative climate have to be altered in his mind.

7. *How does the course fit your industry?* Obviously you will only need to ask this question if you're looking at an external course, but even internal courses need checking for the quality of their departmental mixes. There is a fine line to be drawn here – it helps put one's own problems into perspective if one sees how things are run in other industries, and it helps to question one's own assumptions. But the trainer should at least know something about your own industry – if necessary by asking you – so that he will help the trainee to put unfamiliar points into a familiar perspective. See if you can tell what assumptions the trainer makes about the industry – is he sensitive to the different forms an organisation can take? The different time-scales necessary to react? The different approaches to risk-taking? The impact of different nationalities? If you suspect that he is interpreting the whole world in terms of the organisation he grew up in, or wants to mould the realities of the outside world to fit his own pet theories, go somewhere else.

8. *What stress level will the trainee experience?* You do not want your poor performer's problems made worse by the imposition of unnecessary stress. Stress on courses comes from a number of different factors – not knowing what will happen next, not knowing if one is being assessed, not knowing how well one is doing compared to everyone else, staying up late to finish assignments, eating too much and not getting enough exercise, sitting at a desk all day – and very little of it is likely to help your poor performer's motivation. Try to make sure that people are not exposed to unnecessary stress.

9. *What assumptions are made about the skills and knowledge that the trainees bring to the course?* Check that the course is not attracting too wide an ability range for the trainer to devote his attention equally to all the trainees.

10. *How is the course evaluated?* You need to know whether the trainer is interested in knowing whether his courses work. 'Happiness sheets' distributed at the end of a course are of

limited use in evaluation. If people know what they need to know and can tell when they've got it, then happiness sheets are a good measure of course success. But if people are not so much in command of their own learning needs, for whatever reason, then happiness sheets will just tell you something of their state of mind as they left the course. Ideally, you want answers to the question: 'What are your trainees doing back at the job differently from, or better than, they did before the course?'

11. *Will your course meet my needs?* Show the trainer your own statement of the changes you want to achieve from the course. Ask whether this is a remit he can work to. Pay attention to the questions he asks you about how you arrived at that remit. Is he really interested in it? Does he ask for priorities? Does he say where, if anywhere, he cannot help?

12. *What help do you want from me?* This is really the most important question of all, and it is the one least often asked. Training in courses away from the job fails, when it does fail, mostly because of lack of management support. The trainee needs your help before the course and after it. The trainer should know this and actively seek your support. If he doesn't know how he wants you to help, then maybe he hasn't studied this important interface enough.

Let us look at the problem of course failure a little more closely. Most obviously it happens after the course; many work groups and supervisors have a well-developed technique for killing any good a course may have done: 'Oh, Arthur's back. Well, you can forget that fancy stuff you learned at the training centre, because up here in the plant we're carrying on as before.' Even without this active hostility to courses, which happens at all levels and not just on the shopfloor, things can go wrong in the early days of learning a new skill. This 'results dip' is noticed by anyone who tries a new physical skill – holding the squash racket differently, playing an *arpeggio* using the wrist instead of the elbow. The first few times things go to pieces – the new way is rarely successful from the start. Under pressure for short-term results the temptation is to give up in despair and go back to the old familiar way, maybe resolving to try the new way you learned on the course when things aren't so hectic. But they never stop being hectic, so the new way gets forgotten and the results never improve. The active help of the manager is necessary if this is not to happen. Here are some examples of what we mean by active help:

1. *A supportive atmosphere* for the training; that is, an assumption that training is useful, that everyone needs it, that the training people have something useful to teach.

2. *De-briefing the trainee* when he comes off the course, privately, as soon as possible on return. The manager should ask if he has returned with any formal or informal action plans; what help he needs from the manager to put these into practice; ask to see his notes or the handouts.

3. *Sharing the learning* by asking the trainee, where this is appropriate, to give a brief summary of the course content and what he learned to the rest of the work group at their next meeting. Here the manager can make clear his supportive attitude.

4. *Feedback on behaviour*, not on short-term results. While he is trying the new way of doing things, results will slip temporarily – the results dip. If the manager puts pressure on for short-term results he can drive the trainee back into the old way of doing things. If the manager can look at what the trainee is doing and say: 'Yes, the elements of the new skill are there all right, they just need a bit more practice and co-ordination', and give feedback in these terms, the trainee is likely to persist until he is through the results dip and performing well – and bringing in the results.

Course failure can also be induced before the course. Inadequate notice or inadequate briefing are often to blame here. If it is part of the process which started with the counselling and disciplinary interview, the poor performer should not be completely surprised by his nomination to the course, but you should nonetheless make a point of taking him aside and going through the course programme with him, passing on any useful information you may have gleaned as a result of talking to the trainer. And the notice should be enough to permit him to hand over his responsibilities without worrying that his work or domestic affairs are being sadly neglected.

Additional points about using courses

It sometimes helps to turn the tables on your poor performer and send him away for the opposite course from the one you think he needs. By this we mean that if he is a dreadful salesman he may learn something from a course for buyers in your industry. If he fouls up his performance appraisal interviews he may learn more from a course on how to be appraised. If he causes lots of trouble with the union maybe you should put him on a course designed to help union people deal with management. Somehow people build lots of defences against learning in one direction, but leave themselves completely open if you come at them the other way.

Try not to let particular courses become associated with poor performers. If this happens, people won't want to go as they will see it as a condemnation of themselves from the outset. Equally, you should avoid the situation where people can only go on certain courses if they have proved themselves to be so good they don't need them.

There is a trend today to use outside trainers to design and run in-house courses. Often this gives you the best of both worlds – the experience and perspective of the outsider, but the context of your own business so that you can draw all the examples, exercises, action plans, etc., from your own work. If you know of a number of poor performers who could be helped thus it's worth putting this proposition to the training department. As a solution it becomes more cost-effective the more often you use it, because the development costs all come at the front, and thereafter repetition is cheaper. On this basis it compares well with using an outside training establishment for a series of courses.

In summary, then, you should think about using formal training courses where there is an identifiable lack of knowledge or skill, and maybe a lack of confidence associated with that gap. Training to meet difficulties with attitude or motivation is less likely to succeed unless you can spread it over a long period of time and use peer group pressure. Training to meet goals such as 'interpersonal sensitivity' and 'self-awareness' and similar loosely defined objectives should be regarded with extreme scepticism and should not be considered as the remedy of first resort. All

training needs management support before, during, and afterwards; part of that support is the skill you use in deciding what
sort of training is necessary. With a poor performer you cannot
afford to have him come back from training worse than when he
left.

Summary

Managing poor performance falls into three parts: spotting that there is a problem, understanding the causes of the problem, and attempting a remedy. In this final chapter we shall draw together these three themes with an overview.

Detection demands that the manager takes a detached view of the problem performance – easy if the problem develops quickly, more difficult if it develops over time. Sometimes the signs of poor performance are there if you look for them early, before they cause a costly incident. Among the signs to look for are drops in work quantity or quality; absenteeism, higher accident rates, other forms of withdrawal from work; conflict and deteriorating relationships; dishonesty, stealing, sabotage; lack of delegation, slowness at making decisions, waywardness and emotionality. If the manager periodically does an internal audit of his staff to check their performance levels he is less likely to be surprised by a performance problem deteriorating to the point where something happens that costs money or orders or even lives. This is not merely a matter of prevention being better than cure. If you let a performance problem reach the point of causing a serious incident you will almost certainly have to devote a great deal of time and energy to clearing up after the incident. This means that the problem performer goes unattended, gets reprimanded without being helped, or gets fired when he could perhaps have been retrieved.

The need to take a detached look at staff performance from time to time is one reason why it is worth the line manager tolerating the systems given him to do this with – systems like performance appraisal, territory management diaries, call reporting systems, etc. If he uses these devices well they can help him detect performance problems well in advance of their becoming intractable. Particularly useful are some of the systems for analysing behaviour, like the SPIN approach to sales skill training, where the manager is equipped to analyse the behaviour; this is likely to result in success whereas concentrat-

168

ing on short-term results may be counterproductive in the long run. Most people are not very good at describing interpersonal skills; they are better at describing feelings or end results. So arises the dilemma that while people are more likely to improve if they get feedback about their skills, unless they have a sensitive or trained manager they are likely to get feedback on less relevant topics.

Though we gave as the objective of this book helping the manager who has one or two people working for him who do not pull their weight, rather than helping the manager who has to turn round a whole division, it is appropriate at least to mention that there are some industries where standards of performance are lacking completely, and some organisations where managers have in general no idea of how good or bad they are. Some old specialist industries are like this – parts of the insurance business, railways, some textile firms, some banks. So are parts of national and local government, hospital and school administration, church and charity organisations, some armed forces. Here the requirement to manage has insidiously crept up on people who hitherto have been specialists or administrators. Their specialist or monopoly nature often attracts people for a lifetime career, so that opportunities for comparisons with the outside world are rare. In such industries the manager with one or two problem performers may find that he has to begin somewhat further back in the detection process. He may have to start a process of establishing performance criteria, or reporting relationships, or contingency planning or some other yardstick with which to demonstrate that his people are falling down on the job.

The causes of poor performance are many and various, and while any one case of poor performance probably has more than one cause we separated different causes for the sake of clarity. Summarising the main causes of poor performance:

1. Intelligence is composed of a number of different factors feeding into a central factor. It is possible to be relatively high on one form of intelligence, e.g. verbal ability, and not so good on another form, e.g. mechanical ability; so assumptions about transferability of abilities must be carefully checked. And while it's possible to be too dull and lacking in intelligence to do the job, it's also possible to be too bright to do it

well because boredom sets in or it becomes difficult to delegate.

2. Memory difficulties can happen because of ageing, or
because of overloading the short-term memory, or because of
illness. Far too many jobs put impossible demands on the
short-term memory store, which can really hold only 7 ± 2
units of information at a time; if you ask people to take in
information and output it again continuously you may be
asking too much of them.

3. Lack of job knowledge, often due to poor initial training,
is at the root of some performance problems. 'Sitting next to
Nellie' to be trained only works if Nellie is a good teacher and
knows that that's what she's being paid to do. Often the
induction period doesn't last long enough, so that people
don't have the licence to ask naive questions or find their way
around in a risk-free environment.

4. Stress (a serious mismatch between the job, the person
doing it, and the motivation to do it) causes performance
problems, usually based on variations of the fight/flight
options. All jobs contain an element of stress, because the
link between stress and motivation is so intimate that you
can't have motivation without having the possibility of some
stress. Stress leads to poor performance when the person
concerned manages it badly, for there are healthy and unhealthy ways of coping with stress. It also leads to poor performance when the work situation provides no clear way for the
person to mange his stress in a healthy fashion.

5. Psychiatric problems, such as neurosis and psychosis, and
alcoholism and drug abuse, may be beyond the skill of the
individual manager to diagnose, let alone treat. The sudden
change in personality, not attributable to other obvious factors like work or domestic problems, may be due to one of
these more serious causes. Here the manager's task is to
introduce the person to professional help and try if necessary
through liaison with the professional help to make the working environment as supportive as possible.

6. Motivational problems are complex – so complex that
many respected writers have suggested that we do without the
term as it is meaningless. Certainly it makes little sense to
speak about 'poor motivation' as if there were a psychic petrol
tank that needed filling up. The key notions to grasp are that

people seek to have a satisfactory job *content* and a satisfactory job *context*, but these two things are quite different and you can't trade one for the other. People can motivate themselves much more strongly and consistently than you as an outsider can, so it's better to set up conditions for self-motivation to occur even if this is more difficult and takes longer.

7. Medical conditions, particularly the kind that are not life-threatening but just annoying, sometimes cause poor performance; either the sufferer doesn't detect that he has a problem or he knows but is reluctant to reveal it or ask for your indulgence in its management. People go slogging on with splitting headaches, bad backs, influenza, frightened to ask if they can take time off to recover or get treatment. Yet you wouldn't expect to run your car non-stop without breaks for service and maintenance. Again, the manager's role here is sometimes to persuade the sufferer to seek medical attention, and maybe later to arrange things so that he gets better quickly.

8. Work groups can put pressure on people which leads to poor performance. The self-limiting norms of a work group may get out of hand. Loyalties can be pulled two ways in a strike or go-slow. The group may reject someone it designates as a stranger for reason of sex, age, race, accent, or any other capricious reason. Work group influence is strong; the manager needs to harness it to his own cause.

9. The organisation may itself have a history of tolerating poor standards, so that when you come in as a new manager determined to sweep the boards clean people genuinely don't know what you're talking about. Or there may have been a history of not wanting to cause trouble with the unions which has made top management unwilling to support local managers who want to take initiatives to improve standards.

10. Selection and induction errors may be responsible for the poor performance. You may have simply selected the wrong man, either by looking for the wrong man and finding him, or by looking for the right man but using poor recruiting practices. Or you may find that the induction programme contained so little job satisfaction, or was so irrelevant to the later demands of the job, that it caused performance to decline – and this, especially in times of high employment, will often

result in the person leaving.

11. Working conditions may affect performance by being too hot or too cold, too noisy or too quiet, too dangerous for people to feel confident, too dirty, not convenient for shops and public transport, etc. It's rare for poor working conditions by themselves to cause poor performance – in pioneering manufacturing industries you'll find people working in draughty lock-up garages and loving it. But neglected working conditions can be seen as a token of management apathy, and make the person feel more like a cog in a wheel.

12. Domestic problems may cause poor performance, by putting extra demands upon time and effort. Sometimes firms with inadequate removals policies contribute to domestic problems by not arranging the move of their employee to coincide with, say, the end of a school term of the sale of the family home.

We gave a warning about being seduced into investigating the causes of poor performance at the expense of concentrating on the cure. The cure may not be obvious once you have the diagnosis – and you can't bring about a cure by reversing the signs on the original problem. Among the *remedies* open to the manager we listed:

1. The counselling and disciplinary interview, which should form a part of almost every action programme with a poor performer. The interview involves several stages: discovering and agreeing on performance standards, agreeing that there has been a gap, agreeing who has responsibility for reducing the gap, agreeing how and by when these measures shall take effect, and agreeing a review procedure. And the interview needs a good deal of skill on the manager's part – skill in setting it up, so that he has all the evidence he needs, has checked with all the interested parties, has arranged the surroundings well; skill in asking questions, testing understanding, and summarising. The art is to get him to agree that he has a problem, because at the start of the interview the only thing you're sure of is that *you* have a problem – and to get that problem to hurt him so much that he is anxious for your help in curing it.

2. You may put someone in a new job, if the problem seems to be caused by a mismatch of basic abilities, or inability to

tolerate the working conditions, or inability to get on with the work group. In this case you need to check that he is clear what the standards of performance are in the new job, and check that he is receiving the appropriate training for the new job so that bad habits cannot carry over or develop afresh.

3. You may redesign the job, altering the physical circumstances, or the responsibilities of the person. You may want to alter his responsibilities in order to get more interest and variety, a change of pace (important as a help in stress management), a sense of interdependence within the group, more opportunity to plan the work, or a closed feedback loop so that he sees the effect of his efforts in his results.

4. You may reorganise the whole department or the whole firm. Not that you would reorganise the whole firm just for one problem performer, but you could be seduced away from taking more direct action because you hope that a coming reorganisation will make things better. Reorganisations are the grave of many a hope like this. In an existing firm the inertia in the system means that people tend to relapse into their old ways of doing things – structure reflects function, it doesn't cause it. Most reorganisations need a great deal of thought before going ahead – more than they get at present, or at least a different kind of consideration from what they usually get. And being put in his new position won't change your poor performer, though it may provide you with a safe excuse for instigating some more definite action.

5. Peer group pressure is remarkably successful in helping with performance problems, especially where the problems are due to unhelpful attitudes or badly organised motivation. To work, peer group pressure needs to be slow; and it needs to be seen as peer group pressure, not as the manager leaning on the whole group to lean on Simon. Which means that to get it to work you need subtlety and patience, and you may need to induce these qualities in your own boss if he's leaning on you for quick results.

6. Professional counselling from an outsider may be helpful with certain types of problem, or where you suspect that you yourself may be bound up in the problem to a degree that makes it difficult for you to give disinterested help. Among the outside counsellors you may have doctors, psychiatrists, industrial chaplains, financial counsellors, career and voca-

tional guidance people, and others. There are problems getting the professional counsellor over the threshold and into the organisation, but many firms feel that having an interested outsider available at need is a useful investment.
7. You may send the poor performer away for training. If the training is to work it needs your support before and after, especially over the 'results dip' when people try new skills and are awkward settling down. It needs to be made clear also that assessments are not being made as part of the training course.

We have written this book in the belief that it is possible for the average manager to give direct help to most of the poor performers he will have to manage. We formed the belief after watching some good managers in action; and we pursued the topic when we saw so many managers afraid of taking action on their poor performers. It's more fun to lead a team of well-motivated, successful people, to be sure; but it is possible to turn a potential failure into one of these successes. And it's no fun being a poor performer either. It must be dreadful to spend eight hours a day doing something badly. To get up in the morning knowing that there's more than a fifty per cent chance you'll foul it up. To know that you'll always come in bottom of this particular class. To take the pride in your hobbies that you know in your heart you should also feel in your job. No wonder the iron gets into the soul; no wonder the bitterness grows, the crust of unfeeling develops to hide from oneself the thought that the rest of one's working life will be a failure. As a manager you have to find a pain-free way to remove that crust, discharge the bitterness, and bring back the pride in standards that he is as capable of as you are.

Recommended reading

The single best summary of work on poor performance in industry is to be found in Dunnette's *Handbook of Industrial and Organisational Psychology* (Rand-McNally, 1976). The summary is thorough rather than discursive, perhaps of less help to the line manager in need of something to do now than to the person with more time to research, but it contains many useful insights.

Try to get hold of the series of three books by Eli Ginzberg, *The Ineffective Soldier: Lessons for Management and the Nation* (Columbia University Press, 1959). These books contain some of the best practical application of behavioural science to the problems of poor performance that we have seen. Though written about the military life, the lessons are indeed of relevance to management and the nation – why the series is not more often used we do not know.

Poor military performance attracts more entertaining writing than poor industrial performance. Norman Dixon's *The Psychology of Military Incompetence* (Jonathan Cape, 1976) is full of insightful anecdotes, and practical remedies, which the line manager will find useful.

We mentioned our own books on the design of performance appraisal systems (*Practical Performance Appraisal*, Gower, 1978) and on helping managers learn (*Managing the Manager's Growth*, Gower, 1978). Modesty should forbid going on about them, and had we known that Alan Mumford was about to put pen to paper with his *Making Experience Pay* (McGraw-Hill, 1980) we might have waited a bit; Mumford's book is required reading for any experienced manager wanting to improve his or his people's chances of learning from experience.

The SPIN system for analysing the effectiveness of sales calls, devised by Neil Rackham and the Huthwaite Research Group, has not at the time of writing been put into a book, but a series of articles Rackham wrote in *Marketing* in 1979/80 gives an over-view of their approach.

The Video Arts people, who make those delightful training films starring John Cleese, have produced *'I'd like a word with you'* on the art of the disciplinary interview. It is in all ways an excellent film, and we have found it to be extremely useful in seminars and courses on the problems of managing poor per-formers.

Index